MAKE MORE WORK LESS

With

CASHFLOW

The Step-by-Step Keys to Finding, Acquiring and Maintaining Cashflow Investment Properties

Make More Work Less with Cashflow
The Step-by-Step Keys to Finding, Acquiring and Maintaining
Cashflowing Investment Properties

Published by
10-10-10 Publishing
1-9225 Leslie Street
Richmond Hill
Ontario, Canada
L3B 3H6

For information about special discounts for bulk purchases, please contact 10-10-10 Publishing at 1-888-504-6257.

Printed in the United States of America

ISBN: 978-1-928155-83-6 (Paperback)
ISBN: 978-1-928155-84-3 (E-book)

First Edition

MAKE MORE WORK LESS

With

CASHFLOW

The Step-by-Step Keys to Finding, Acquiring and Maintaining Cashflow Investment Properties

Fong Chua & Jessica Ng

- ABOUT THE AUTHORS -

Assurance Real Estate Acquisitions Inc. was brought together by the managing partners, Jessica Ng and Fong Chua, to bring to life their beliefs in adding value to people. This partnership specializes in uniting the right people, the right project and the right solution, all while adding value to all those involved, creating a win-win environment. Assurance Real Estate Acquisitions Inc. places great emphasis on relational capital, which is why we treat our clients and partners the same as our loved ones.

Starting out as engineers and winners of the Deal Makers Award, Fong and Jessica have the technical skills and attention to details to ensure that all projects are of value for all parties involved. We have many insider relationships with investors and agents, which allows us to have access to great deals first. Our philosophy is simple, we don't acquire properties unless they are below market value and we don't speculate on appreciation. When it comes to partnerships, three words describe our focus: loyalty, relationships and results. This is why we believe that partners should be for life and why we treat our partner's money even more conservatively than with our own.

Our Mission: To bring wealth, be it financial, knowledge or security, to all those who seek it. With our expertise and heart, it is our mission to impact as many people as we can by showing them how they can achieve more than they think.

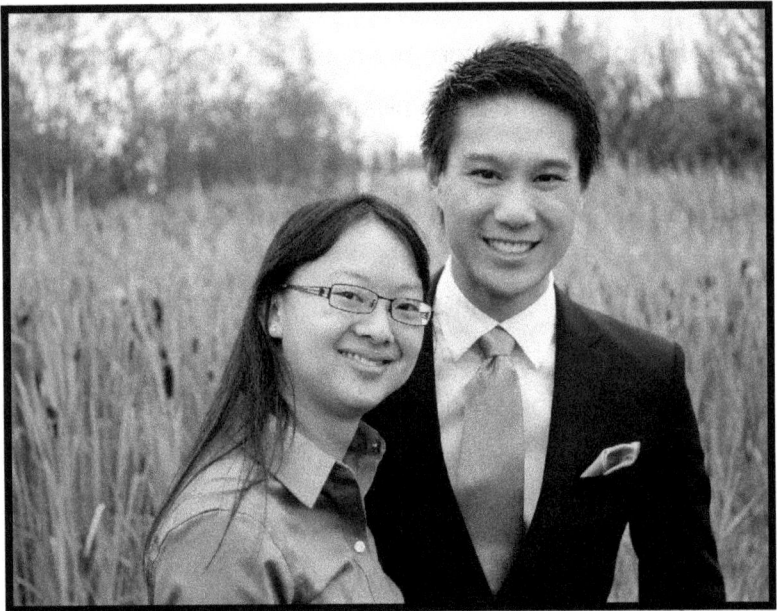

This book is dedicated to:

Our team members, for their great work and assistance with our many successes. During our ventures we have learned many lessons from them whether in the industry or in life – ethics and the meaning of hard work. If not for these characteristics, we would not have had the foundation that got us to where we are today.

Our coach, Shawn Shewchuk, who inspires, motivates and believes in us. He reminds us each day that we can achieve all our goals.

Each other, without the support and the dedication that we committed to our business and to each other, our ventures would not be possible.

- ACKNOWLEDGEMENTS -

We would like to acknowledge and thank all those involved with the publishing of this book for their hard work and care in putting this book together. We are absolutely thankful for their patience and time spent dealing with our requests.

Thank you to everyone that supported us in this venture: from writing, to editing (Louise Harris, LAST Research & Editing), to cover design (Jong Chua, Just Creative Inc.), to photography (Wilson Wong, Everbrave Branding Group Ltd.), to guidance (Shawn Shewchuk, Coach) and assistance. Your assistance, support and motivation are deeply appreciated. We would also like to extend a heartfelt thank you to our circle of loving family, friends, clients and peers who have all been very supportive and encouraging to us.

Finally, we cannot thank Shawn Shewchuk enough for his friendship and phenomenal support during this venture. Thank you Shawn for your belief in us and for writing the foreword to this book.

- CONTENTS -

- FOREWORD -

For nearly two decades, I have studied and worked with individuals and corporations from around the world. When I met Jessica and Fong, I knew there was something different about them. I knew that they would make a difference in the world. When I read this book, it all came together, it made sense. I understood how they were going to have a far-reaching impact.

I've had the honor of knowing and working with Jessica and Fong for nearly three years. In that time, I have witnessed phenomenal transformation and positive growth in them both. The reason? They took the necessary steps to get to where they wanted to go. They acted on and executed the extremely important and detailed processes that they have outlined in this book.

The information contained between these covers is vital to your life and professional aspirations. There are many people that have a deep desire to obtain this information. There are many that want to do what you are about to do, but lose courage and fear chokes out their chances for success. You see, you cannot place a value on this information, it is invaluable if utilized correctly. Know this, you can become anything that you desire, you can build your business as big as you like, but it will not be what you may consider as easy. There may be stumbling blocks, use these as stepping stones and keep climbing.

As a result of taking the action steps that are an absolute necessity, and as outlined in this book, Jessica and Fong are now successful business people. This power couple is leading the way to entrepreneurial success through an easy to follow step-by-step process. More importantly, Jessica and Fong are leaders through their impressive examples of tenacity and positively presumptuous aspirations.

There is a vast difference between those that talk about doing something of substance, and those that go out when they are unable to find the situation that they want, create something that they want, something that fosters passion and leaves a legacy of significance. Just as Jessica and Fong have achieved through following these simple but powerful steps, you can sail right through your targets as well.

This book will become a resource that you will turn to again and again for inspiration and information. This is your handbook to achieving the dreams and objectives of your life and business. You need only make an irrevocable decision to follow what Jessica and Fong have proven as successful, and take immediate action. You are now in possession of the manual, and execution is the key.

If you will prepare yourself for change, understand the concepts and universal principles that have been diligently outlined by Jessica and Fong, you too will experience extra-ordinary results.

Shawn Shewchuk
Bestselling author and
The No.1 Results Coach in the Country

- INTRODUCTION -

Long ago, Fong and I had gone to our first real estate event. We were excited to attend our first three-day event to learn what we needed to do to start on our path to financial freedom via real estate. We dreamt about how we would no longer have to worry about losing our engineering jobs should the oil and gas industry plummet; about how we can help our families, especially the ones overseas or those that aren't well off; and how we can finally make a bigger and better impact on our community. Things were going to be great!

During the three-day course, we had learned so much. We realized there was still so much we needed to know to get us to where we wanted to be. We had no idea that there was so much to real estate. We knew we needed more education to get us where we wanted to be. To help our families, friends and community and to live life on our own terms, not what our bosses tell us to do. We were scared out of our minds. We had just signed up for what we felt was a HUGE expense to learn the advanced techniques of real estate investing. It didn't matter though, our dreams and desires told us it was the right thing to do.

As we continued to learn about real estate over the years, we have now reached a level where we are comfortable with finding, maintaining and most of all, profiting from cashflowing properties. Looking back, we were SHOCKED to see how much time and money we spent on courses and books. If only we had a book that told us everything we should be doing to get good

3

cashflow properties. Just one book, instead of the multiple books we had to read to be where we are today. Since we haven't found a good book that covers almost everything one would need to know to get good cashflowing properties, we decided to unlock the secrets we have learned over the years by writing this book *Make More Work Less with Cashflow* for you.

We have split this book into three sections:
1) Mindset
2) Acquiring Properties
3) Maintaining Relationships and Properties

In the first section, we will talk about mindset. We realized that although we were keen on reaching our dreams, our mindset at the time wouldn't allow us to succeed. Growing up in a Chinese culture, we believed that we had to get good grades and get a good job, which we did! This mindset of just working hard our entire life in a "stable" job wasn't enough to let us dream the big dreams of real estate. It wasn't the right mindset if one wanted to Make More and Work Less. So before we could reach our dreams, we had to work on our mindset first, to allow it to expand and think big.

In the second section, we will talk about acquiring properties. As many gurus will tell you, you make money in the buy, not the sell. What this means is that if you buy the property at the right price, you will win each time. It is not when you sell the property that you make money, but when you buy it right. When you learn to buy a property at the right price and learn the things to look for and anticipate problems that could arise, you can minimize your own risk.

4

In the third section, we will talk about relationships, networking and maintaining the property. Relationships are especially important as we all like dealing with people we like. When you focus first on how you can help others, you will find that success will follow. Whether it is helping an investor make more money, or a tenant to find a good home, you will feel great knowing that you have provided some value to others. Building great relationships is essential if you want to Make More and Work Less with Cashflow. As an extension to relationship, it is important to maintain the property as well. With a good property, tenants will have no complaints and in turn, neither will your investor!

What we want to provide to you, our valued reader today, is a comprehensive guide to getting and maintaining cashflowing properties with practical tips that we have learned over these years. We sincerely hope to help you achieve your dreams without having to spend the same amount of time and money that we have spent. It is our hope also that you will use your newfound skills to help your community and those in it. As Napoleon Hill put it, "It is literally true that you can succeed best and quickest by helping others succeed." Now, let's get into the keys of the book so you can Make More and Work Less with Cashflow!

Thank you and enjoy!

- SECTION 1 -

Mindset and Preparation

You will probably find that most of the people around you think that you are CRAZY for thinking about becoming an investor. The truth is that with respect to the general public- YOU ARE! It is the 'crazy' people that change the world and become successful. To that, we would like to congratulate you for taking that step forward and joining the top 1 percent. You've taken the first step in deciding to make a difference in your life, and there is more to come. To become successful in investing, the most important key is your MINDSET. Without the correct mindset you will be missing a key component to what is needed to become successful. You must begin to train yourself to see more than the average person; to think bigger than the everyday person; to think transformationally instead of transactionally; and to act in a diagonal manner instead of just vertically or horizontally. You must feed your mind daily so that your brain will trigger when the opportunity presents itself. Just as an athlete constantly trains so that their response time is quicker, so must we to seize the keys to an opportunity when it comes. If we act too slowly, the ball will already be in someone else's hands.

Have you ever noticed that once you buy a certain brand of car, you see it everywhere on the street? You start thinking to yourself, *"How come I've never seen so many before?"* Well, the reason is that you are bombarded with tons of information daily. For you to function, your brain filters out what it feels is unimportant to you. Once you have bought your car, you have just unlocked an area of your mind that tells you that your brand of car is important. Suddenly, that is all you notice. This concept applies to everything, including investing. Once you have used the keys in this section to unlock the investing part of your mind, you will be prepared to see opportunities and seize it. The more you think "Make More Work Less with Cashflow" the more you will seize those opportunities.

"There is no such thing as impossible dreams, only unrealistic time lines."

- Nido Qubein -

Chapter - 1 -

Mindset:

You Are What You Think

You were born to win, but to be a winner:
you must plan to win, prepare to win
and expect to win.

- Zig Ziglar -

A couple of our friends, John and Melissa, approached us recently saying: "We've been looking at our lives and our finances and where we want to be. And truthfully, there is no way of getting where we want with the financial situation we are in. We've been looking at other sources of income and have found that real estate investing is the only one that makes the most sense. However, we don't know the first thing about investing. This is a big realization for us and frankly it's a little scary. We don't really know what we are getting ourselves into. Since you two have been successful in investing, we were hoping that you can give us some advice."

MAKE MORE WORK LESS with CASHFLOW

Within the pages of our *Make More Work Less: The Guide to Unlocking Your Potential to Live and Work on Your Own Terms,* we talked about the importance of mindset and how to train it. We will go over some aspects of it here and also provide a few other examples of having the right MINDSET.

What you put into your body is what you will get from it. The effort you put into something is directly related to the results that you get. If you study hard for an exam you will most likely come out of that exam successful. In contrast if you waited until the last day to study, then chances are great that you will not have done very well on that exam. Same can be said about how you think. If you think positively, then more positive situations will come to you. Similarly if you think negatively, more unfortunate things will occur.

Have you ever gotten out of bed and felt tired and prefer to go back to sleep? Knowing that you have to go to work, you don't have a choice but to rise. Already you feel negative about the notion of not being able to go back to sleep. As the day progresses, the traffic feels extra slow (no slower or faster than it was every other day), and for some reason it felt slower than usual. When you get to work it seemed like finding a spot was harder than usual. Now, you are thinking *"Boy! Am I having a bad day!"* You get to the elevator and just as you get to the doors...they close. You finally get to your office and realize that the coffee pot is empty and you now need to wait for a new pot to brew. By now, you really feel that you are having a bad day. That feeling brews inside of you and throughout the rest of the day all these negative things seem to appear. More problems

11

than usual, your favorite donut is sold out. You feel more tired and start getting a headache. And so it continues until you get home. The entire day you were grumpy and people start to avoid you and you feel that you are being ignored and that the day is getting worse and worse. Truth is...the day is no different than any other day, but the moment you felt negative about not getting more sleep, it completely changed how you usually perceive things.

When you feel positive you may have thought "Great, I can get more things done today if I get to the office a little early!" or "huh...I missed the elevator...maybe I'll take the stairs and get some exercise." All of a sudden, more and more positive viewpoints come to you. People approach you more and conversations are lively and fun. All that is different is what you thought. Henry Ford once said *"Whether you think you can, or you think you can't – You're right."* So why do we not think more about success and opportunity?

Unfortunately, humans have been brought up to attract and to be accepting of bad stuff. News with high ratings is news about disasters, conflict, or controversies in the world. People just don't respond to happy news the same way. Even if it was good news like someone winning the lottery, chances are you are thinking *"How come I can't win the lottery...Life is not fair!"* changing the emotions of what should be happy news into negative news. Therefore, media keeps informing us about the bad news. The more we are exposed to negative news, the more we notice it and view things in a negative perspective. How can we stop this behavior? It is all in our minds. However, this is easier said than done. There are certain things one can do to assist us to be more positive. The more effort you put into being positive, the easier it becomes. Thinking positive is no different than exercising a muscle. The more we exercise it, the stronger it is. By being more positive, we will start noticing more opportunities that are there, rather than listen to all the naysayers around us.

To help us remember to remain positive and open to opportunities rather than to negativity and obstacles, we have created an acronym: CAP

C: Confidence
A: Attitude
P: Persistence

Let's explore these a little more closely now.

Confidence

Confidence is something that usually stops us from doing the things we want to do. When we want to do something, we would go find out what skills we would need and put in the time to learn it. However most of us would then start doubting ourselves. Can I really do this? What if I do it wrong? What if I don't know enough?

How can we avoid this? Well, people build confidence by doing it. You learn the skills, practice it and apply it. To help you understand how we build confidence, we will explain the four levels that we all go through when developing confidence. The first level is unconscious incompetence, the second is conscious incompetence, the third level is conscious competence and the last level is unconscious competence.

1 – Unconscious Incompetence
2 – Conscious Incompetence
3 – Conscious Competence
4 – Unconscious Competence

In our *Make More Work Less: The Guide to Unlocking Your Potential to Live and Work on Your Own Terms,* we used the example of driving. Let's look at it in a sporting aspect – golf. As we went through life, we didn't know anything about golf. That's unconscious incompetence. Another way of putting this is, you don't know what you don't know.

As we grew up, we realized that golf was something people go and play. We didn't know how to hold the clubs, what clubs to use, how to stand or how score is kept. We also realized how many people enjoy golf and decided to look more into it and that we could also one day go "play" golf, it's not just for business people or athletes, but we also can golf, but we just don't know how. Now we have reached the second level of conscious incompetence. We know what we don't know, but we don't know how to do it yet. This is why you need to practice.

In this example, most of us would go and get clubs or rent clubs and find a coach or an instructor. Soon enough, we will technically know how to: swing, keep score and putt. Now, we have learned the skills we need to play golf and have reached the third level of conscious competence. We still need to think about how to actually swing and the procedure of having proper placement, but we have the necessary skills required to play golf.

Finally, as we continue to apply our skills and keep playing golf and practice at the driving range, it will become so second nature that our bodies just knows what to do. We no longer have to think "feet shoulder length apart, head down, knees bent etc." we just do it. This level is unconscious competence.

Once we are competent, we need to stop doubting ourselves and simply trust that we are able to do it. You didn't give up on walking when you were a toddler just because you weren't sure of yourself did you? We know you had just kept practicing until you were more comfortable. Anything we do in life is like that. Just as you trust that you can walk, you should trust in your abilities to learn the skills you need and apply it, regardless if it is golf, or anything else you set your mind to.

Attitude

Confidence is not the only thing we require to help our mindset. Having good attitude is another key. How do I get that? The key is in your thoughts. As we have discussed before, the more you exercise thinking positively, the easier it will get. But how do we even start thinking positively in the first place? It is all in your attitude and how you think about incidents.

A story about positive attitude that comes to mind was told to us by Dr. Nido Qubein:

A grumpy businessman on a plane was waiting for the sandwiches to be served for lunch. The man took a bite, looked up at the assistance button and rang it like rapid fire. The flight attendant, Mandy, came running down the aisle and asked the man "What seems to be the problem?" The man glares up at her and screams, "This is a BAD sandwich!" Mandy looks at the man, picks up his sandwich and says, "Bad sandwich! Bad sandwich!" and slapped the sandwich with her other hand. Mandy handed the sandwich back and left promptly as the passengers nearby snickered and the man remain quiet and beet red. After the plane landed, one of the passengers stayed behind and waited for the flight attendant that punished the sandwich and asked, "What in your mind prompted you to do such a thing while dealing with such a jerk of a passenger?" With that, the flight attendant replied "Well. I deal with passengers like that all the time, and, if I was to let them get to me, I would start to hate my job, complain to my fellow co-workers and can't wait to retire." After hearing this answer, the passenger could imagine that after Mandy beat the sandwich she must have hastily gone to the back holding in her laughter and said to her co-worker, "Hey Jill, You wouldn't believe what I did to the passenger in 7D..." in which laughter will ensue. Mandy will now have a great story to tell her friends and family, loving her job as each day passes.

When you read that story, can you see the difference of attitude Mandy has compared to what others may have had? Could you imagine the fun and enjoyment that she has while doing her job? Most of us would be mad at a situation that we felt we were being attacked, but, if we were to have a fun attitude, the situation would not be as bad as we first thought. Why not just skip the rollercoaster emotion and look for the good in what we may think is a bad situation at the time? By doing so, you could possibly see a hidden opportunity when most people would only see an obstacle.

Persistence

Do you remember learning to ride a bike when you were young? If you don't, maybe you have kids and recently taught your kids to ride a bike. You start on a tricycle, then a bicycle on training wheels and then finally took those wheels off and now riding a bicycle. There isn't one person that jumped on a bike and rode it instantly, chances are great they fell over the first few times and scraped their knees, cried, or complained about how hard it was and that it is impossible. Still, you would try again and again because you wanted to be able to ride a bike. Your parents or guardians would be encouraging you to do it and cheer for you.

At times you just want to give up, but because of the people cheering you on and you wanting to ride, you would try again and again. Finally, with more practice and persistence, you learned the tricks of the trade to riding a bike. Now, riding a bike is natural to you that you don't even have to tell yourself, "hands on the handle bars, get on the seat, push with your feet...balance and PEDAL!" No, you can now ride without thinking.

After all these years, you've grown up. Unfortunately, people in general are negative and fearful of new things that they don't understand. Misery attracts misery, if they can't do something, people will tell you how you can't do something. If you have people to encourage you to do the things you want to do then great, but if not, your attitude and confidence is even more important to get you where you want to be. When things get hard and more people tell you that you can't, it is persistence that gets you to your goals.

Ultimately one key point that we want to unlock is what is your "WHY". Why do you want to do something? Why are you working on this goal? Why is this so important to you? Why keep going if it's so hard? Why did you wake up this morning? Why, why, why. The WHY is what will keep pushing you when things are looking bleak and you want to give up and your attitude and confidence in yourself is no longer enough. If your why doesn't make your heart soften, then keep working on finding it.

Your why is your mission, it is the foundation of what you are building in your life. A weak foundation will result in having goals that will falter in a matter of time. A strong foundation will stand tall no matter what comes at you. A great saying that we live by is *"No matter the wind, rain, snow or sleet, we will stand tall, push forward and succeed."*

Having a great mindset that is susceptible to opportunities rather than barriers and remembering the acronym CAP: Confidence, Attitude and Persistence, will lead you to believe in yourself, think positively and most of all: trust in your mission.

To assist you in doing so, there are little tricks that you can do to encourage you to work towards your WHY. We will show you 3 different levels of strategies.

Beginner: Vision board
Intermediate: Mindfeed (books and audios)
Advanced: Mastermind group and a plan

Vision Board

Pictures can do wonders to what you attract. Having your goals constantly reminded in your mind's eye will help you focus on what you need to do. A vision board is a board with pictures and words on it to help you visualize your goals. This board should be placed somewhere that you will see all the time as a reminder for yourself. Either on your bathroom mirror, where you keep your keys or by your TV, as long as it is somewhere you will see everyday. Because you bought this book, we will assume that one of your goals is to have cashflowing properties. Put a picture of that on your board; however, vision boards are not just materialistic items. Remember we discussed your why? Your vision board should have that too. When times are hard, look at your vision board to give yourself the strength to continue. Look at your why and what you want to achieve everyday, and you will eventually achieve what you remind your mind's eye everyday. What goes on a vision board? We suggest the following but by all means not limited to:

- Family/Friends
  - Where do you see yourself with your family and friends?
  - Are there certain things you want to accomplish with them?
  - Who are the people you care about most?

- Financial
  - Where do you see yourself financially?
  - How many cashflowing properties do you see yourself owning?
  - Are there charities or causes that you want to support?

- Fun
  - Where do you want to go?
  - What do you want to have?
  - What do you want to do?

- Mental
  - Are there things you wish to learn?
  - What are some things you want to do to keep your mind active?
  - What new skill do you want to possess?

- Physical
  - Where do you see yourself physically and health wise?
  - Are there things you see yourself doing that you can't do now?
  - What foods should you want to eat?
  - Do you want to gain or lose weight?

- Spiritual
  - o Are there places you want to travel to rejuvenate your spirit?
  - o What are things you want to accomplish to keep your spirit high?

Each vision board is unique to the person. Some categories may not apply to you, while other categories might not apply to others. Feel free to explore the possibilities of your vision board and to make it something you believe in yourself.

The more you see it, the more your mind will be "looking" for opportunities that bring those items to you. Instead of thinking that the items are dreams or far-fetched goals, your mind will slowly believe that you already are in possession of the items in your vision board.

An example of a great vision board is: wanting your dream car. Say for instance you want a car which will cost you $40K. You know that you can save $1666 a month. As you save the money each month you put on your vision board a slice of the picture of your dream car. Every month you add to the picture 4 percent at a time. By the end of one year, you will see half of your car on your board. Seeing your dream car materialize in front of your eyes will keep you going. At times, it may even push you to work harder or smarter to get to the full car as you see it getting closer and closer. Soon enough you will be driving what you already owned in your mind a long time ago.

A great story about a powerful vision is that of Walt Disney. After the completion of Disneyland in Anaheim

California, Walt was disappointed about all the hotels and stores that were built around Disneyland, he felt that it took away from the magic of Disney. So he set off on a dream to build Disney World! After years of complications, land purchases and development, Disney World was finally completed. Sadly, Walt Disney passed away long before Disney World was completed. During the opening ceremony of Disney World, Roy, Walt's brother who came out of retirement to fulfill his brother's dream was asked: *"Isn't it unfortunate that Walt isn't here today to see Disney World completed?"* Roy answered *"Walt saw Disney World completed long before he passed away, that is why we see it now."* That is the power of vision in your mind.

Mindfeed

You are what you eat. Just like how we need to feed our bodies healthily for it to function efficiently, we must also feed our minds. Efficient mindfeeding is feeding your mind with positive and stimulating things. Instead of watching TV and listening to the radio, consider reading or listening to a business book or something related to what you want to be. There are many books and audio books out there that can feed us with uplifting stories or remind us of why we are doing what we are doing. Not only that, there are many books and audios that enhance or teach us new skills. What do you allow into your mind?

Remember the "Bad Day" story we talked about before? We fed ourselves ideas and stories of negative things that ultimately cause us to attract bad things to happen. It is this aspect that makes mind feeding very important.

Feed your mind with inspiration, motivation and information that will enrich your mind, and, in doing so, you will live feeling inspired, motivated and attracting the feelings and opportunities that you have been feeding your mind. We should mind feed everyday for about 30 minutes to an hour first thing in the morning. How else should you start your day if you don't start it positively?

As we have mentioned in our book *Make More Work Less*, most people think garbage in means garbage out. Nido Qubein tell us that it is actually when garbage gets in your mind, it doesn't just go out, it gets pregnant and gives birth to triplets! So be careful what you let in your mind. Be selective about it and ensure that it supports the goals you have set for yourself on your vision board.

Mastermind Group

The purpose of a mastermind group is to draw together like-minded individuals. The group reinforces the growth and success of the individuals in the group while offering support to each other. People gain power by sharing knowledge, visualizing goals, and connecting each other with resources that might not otherwise be available to an individual of the group. Anyone can set up a mastermind group as long as they know like-minded people.

Have you ever noticed that it is more exciting to go watch a football game when everyone is cheering for that same team? Or watching a scary movie is more fun when watching with others who like scary movies? It is because you all have the same goals, likes and passion. You might not like the opinions your friends have about certain players on a sports team, but you both want them to win. Debating about the true meaning of a movie or certain scenes that you liked is more fun when you have someone to debate with who liked the movie as well but had different opinions. Not only that, you might learn or see things a little differently after hearing what your partner had to say. Likewise, with a mastermind group, by having discussions about what is working and what is not, allows everyone to enjoy what they are doing and at the same time, learn from everyone else and grow together.

To grow in a group you must not be the smartest person in the group. If this is the case, what will end up happening is that you would constantly teach the people in your group. Everyone is growing except for you. The best and most powerful group is that everyone has the same mindset and goals in life in general, but as individuals are very diverse in skills, experiences and abilities. That way everyone has something to offer to the group. Everyone is an expert in a certain area and can teach that aspect while at the same time can learn different aspects from the others in the group, allowing everyone to grow.

Imagine this group like it is a personal support group and that you are there to support each person. Push each other to strive for more and assist each other as much as possible. This mastermind group also can hold you accountable for your actions as well. For example, if you said you were going to stop eating fast foods, they will be checking with you to ensure you are on your way to reach your goal.

Your mastermind group is a great source for accountability. Having people holding you accountable is an added bonus of a mastermind group. Accountability and challenging each other are what allows everyone to grow within the group. Not only will it be competitive within the group when people are being kept on track but it also can be a lot of fun as well. Together, the group can find the strengths and weaknesses and also what methods will motivate them the most. For example, having awards and friendly punishments for achievements accomplished or not can be a fun method of motivation.

One of our favorite stories about having an accountability group is one where both parties are striving to cut down eating sweets. If one was to submit to their cravings and satisfy their sweet tooth, then they will need to clean the other person's bathroom! Talk about motivation!

Great ideas, opportunities and enjoyment will arise when you are collaborating with members of your mastermind group. Ultimately, you will be amazed at what such a group can accomplish!

Plan

Planning is one of the key components to success. What would it be like if someone told you to go to a small town in South Africa without giving you a map? You will most likely get lost! This is the same thing that you are doing to yourself, if you do not plan out how you are going to achieve what it is you want to achieve.

Let's say you want to have a book written by the end of November. What must you do to get there? How many chapters should you be writing? How long will editing take? How long will designing a book cover be? When will you need to send it to a publisher? When should you have an outline set? Work backwards from your goals and you will have a plan. Just remember, as George S. Patton once said, *"A good plan violently executed now is better than a perfect plan executed next week."* So just start with a plan now and adjust it as you move along.

Set yearly, monthly and daily goals and activities. Review your goals everyday and plan what you want to accomplish the next day. This will allow you to wake up ready to go! You will have a plan as to what you need to do and when you need to finish it.

Remember back in university or college when the professor tells you that you'll have a paper due on the 30th? When do you start writing that paper? 28th? 29th? The morning of the 30th? What happens if the paper is moved to the 10th of the next month? Would you start now? What would it be like if you planned ahead and set aside some time every day to research, compile the materials, write a page or so a day? Would you be anxious as to when the paper is due? Would you need to stay up all night writing and scrambling to get it done? Devising a plan allows you to focus and manage your energy and time. You will no longer be wasting time thinking of what you need to do or if you have forgotten anything.

Most people have trouble setting goals correctly. People need to strive for something. Goal-setting allows for that. However, many goals are not reached due to people's inability to set goals correctly. The three most common errors people make while goal setting are: Goal is too unachievable. It is too vague. They have no timeline. Let's look at these problems in detail and find out how we can avoid these mistakes.

When deciding on a goal it is very important to set something that is not impossible. Challenging and outside your comfort zone is important and different than impossible. For example, if your goal for this year is to run a marathon, when you haven't done any running before in your life, then a goal to complete a marathon next week without any training would not be recommended or even possible. However, a goal of completing a marathon in six months, although outside your comfort zone may be challenging and doable for you. To make that goal even more realistic is to set three levels of a goal: level one to complete a 10K run in two months. Level two: complete a half marathon in four months and finally level three: to complete a full marathon in six months. On top of that, each time you reach a goal you will be more motivated to reach the next level.

Setting a goal that is not specific and detailed will result in uncompleted goals. For example, if one were to say: "I want a car." What does that mean? What kind? How many? Does buying a toy car count? Are you building one? Renting one? Buying one? Leasing one? etc. However, if one were to say "I want a four-door sedan Toyota Corolla, royal blue with leather seats, sports edition by Aug. 25, 2014," then, we know exactly what you want and when you will achieve that goal.

Without a timeline, nothing ever gets done. Just think about the last thing you wanted to do like cleaning out the garage. Next week, I will clean it, but it started raining, so you figured you can do it the following week. Then you forgot, or you just didn't feel like it. Without even noticing, summer and fall passed and winter came which is not garage-cleaning weather. Without dates and commitment to those dates, things that you wanted to do will always get pushed back. Having dates will allow you to work backwards and set smaller goals. By the first, I will have the left corner of the garage cleaned. By the third, the right corner and so on. Soon enough, you will see that getting the job done is easier. Chances are great after you finish cleaning the left corner, you realized that it only took you 15 minutes. Because you are already dressed in cleaning clothes, you start cleaning the right corner. As you see the garage slowly showing improvement, you will get more and more excited about getting it done.

Planning and strategizing becomes easier once you have your goals and plan in place. At first, it may seem a huge undertaking, but the goal setting and help of a mastermind group, coach, mentor and supportive family and friends, will make achieving your plans easier. A great program that we recommend is Raymond Aaron's monthly mentor. His goal-setting techniques are second to none.

Setting goals and achieving them are a vital part of success. But, this is not a goal-setting book, so we can't go into more detail on how to set or achieve goals. However, our mentor and friend Raymond Aaron has written a bestselling hardcover book *Double Your Income Doing What You Love*, recognized as the world's No. 1 authority on goal-setting achievement. In fact, on the back cover, there are testimonials from giant celebrities who use his program. One such testimonial is by Jack Canfield, the co-creator of the *Chicken Soup For The Soul* series of books. Here is his testimonial: *"The reason I personally chose to use this amazing system for myself and for my company is that, bluntly stated, it is the most powerful system ever created."* By special arrangement, we have permission to allow you, our dear reader, to own a copy of Mr. Aaron's book for free and you can get it by instant download simply by going to his website, www.aaron.com.

After looking at how Confidence, Attitude and Persistence affects one's mindset and how we can utilize the power of a vision board, the advantages of mind feeding, the dynamics of a mastermind group and the benefits of planning and goal setting, we hope that you are on your way to developing a mindset geared towards fulfilling your dreams to Make More and Work Less with Cashflow.

A great book on mindset is written by our coach Shawn Shewchuk, *Change your Mind, Change Your Results - #1 Proven Success Strategies*. We had the privilege of working with Mr. Shewchuk and can say without a doubt that his book and his teachings have changed our mindsets to seek opportunities, results and success. Feel free to contact us for more information.

**Think and believe that your vision will come true.
That is the first step in reaching your dreams.**

Chapter 1 – Mindset: You Are What You Think

Whether you think you can or whether you think you can't, you are right.

- Henry Ford -

Assurance Keys to Your Success

- Confidence – believe in yourself

- Attitude – think positively

- Persistence – trust in your mission

- Create a vision board

- Mind feed with quality that promotes your vision

- Start a mastermind group to support your goals

- Grow with your group and be accountable

- Create your personal plan to success

- Set goals that are achievable yet challenges you

- Manage your time and energy effectively

Chapter - 2 -

Dress for Success

Act Like You Belong

Don't fake it till you make it, act like you belong.

- J.T. Foxx -

"My mindset is on the right path, but what can I do now to feel and act successful? Thinking is one thing, doing is completely another thing. What is the first thing that we should do?" asked John. To get them started in feeling confident and successful, we showed them the first step.

33

Do You Judge a Book by its Cover?

You know the saying: "Never judge a book by its cover"? Unfortunately, the truth is we all do. We as human beings are attracted to the shinier of two things, the cleaner of two items or the bigger of two piles. When it comes to business and relationships, we also apply the same thought process. Next time, you go meet your banker or your lawyer, imagine what it would be like if he or she was wearing coveralls and a sweatshirt. Think about how you first met your accountant or property manager. What was your initial impression? What did you feel? And parents, think about that first time you met your children's significant other or the one who no longer is in the picture. We all experience these situations one way or another and before we know it, we already have a judgment as to who they are. We ask, *"Are they capable? Are they ethical?"* But, how can one tell based on looks whether a person is efficient at their jobs or worthy of your daughter's love? We can't and therefore, if we are forced to do it, we will then get to know a certain person and hope that he or she can prove your first instinct wrong or right. However, if the impression is negative to start, it is an uphill battle from the get-go for you to change your mind. Why do so many "business" owners not treat their businesses like a business – professionally? Dress like successful people, i.e. treat your business like a business. By doing so, you will act and feel like someone who will Make More and Work Less.

No matter how much we don't like it, the way you dress has a big factor on your success and prosperity. Why? Opportunities will come to you depending on the way you look, the way you act and the way you think. It is true that the opposite occurs as well -- where a person who presents themselves well, clean and professionally may or may not be all they seem to be, but, at least, your initial impression of them is high. It is human nature to be more forgiving and more patient when you have a 'good feeling' about something. You are looking for the positive things instead of the negative things. You are on a mission to prove to yourself that your initial 'gut' instinct is correct and that they are, in fact, great people! So knowing this much why wouldn't you dress for success? If by simply dressing professionally, puts you at an advantage why wouldn't you do so? The fact that the way we dress affects how we feel, how we act and ultimately how others see us, makes dressing for business the first action we all should take.

How Do You FEEL?

Remember when you first went on a date or went to your first job interview? What did you do? What did you wear? Did you spend hours or days thinking of which suit to wear or which shoes to match? When you finally reduced your choices to your final two outfits, what ultimately became your deciding factor? Probably it was how it made you feel while wearing it. Why do we do that? It is because we know that if we didn't feel "good" or "confident" or "comfortable" in what we are wearing, it will show through our actions while we are wearing it. How we feel has a lot to do with how successful we can be. If something is too tight or something you wear reminds you of a negative memory, you will subconsciously remember those things or concentrate on how tight your outfit is, taking you away from what is important at the moment - to impress. How do you feel when you put on your favorite jacket or sling your most loved handbag over your shoulder? Do you feel down? Of course not! You feel like you are on top of the world and that you have a purpose. When you see yourself in the mirror with that sharp looking suit or your freshly shined boots, you can't help but smile at yourself. Your smile shows confidence and determination. You feel more confident and feel more determined when you see the confidence and determination in yourself.

Let's try a little demonstration. Guys, go pick out your best looking suit, dress shirt, belt, shoes, a tie and an everyday T-shirt. Ladies, find your most prized suit jacket, blouse, skirt, shoes and a pair of flip flops. Now guys, put on everything, but your dress shirt. Instead, put on your T-shirt and your tie. Look in the mirror and on a scale of one through ten, ten being AWESOME and one being 'yuck', how do you feel? Ladies, same with you, put on everything but your stylish boots. Instead, put on your flip flops. Now how do you feel? What do you notice the most? The everyday T-shirt and flip flops? You can't seem to ignore them regardless of how nice all the other things you have on are. You feel incomplete and "off," like something isn't right. How confident do you feel at this moment? Do you feel like you can close a deal? Get hired for a job? Win the heart of your loved one? Remember these feelings and now fix what needs to be fixed. Notice that you instantly know what needs to be fixed and can't wait to fix it. Now that your shiny boots are on and your flip flops are off, how do you feel? Guys, do you want to put that T-shirt back on? Of course not. You are too busy posing like 007 himself. Now how do you feel? How's that job opening now? As good as closed! At this moment you may feel like you are on top of the world, but wait there is more. Guys, find a handkerchief, or some white cloth, or even (if you really can't find one) a piece of paper. Fold it up in to a triangle and now stuff it into your outer chest suit pocket with a corner of the handkerchief, cloth or paper sticking from the pocket. NOW how do you feel? An 11? 12? Awesome right? Gals, take out that simple yet elegant necklace that you have stashed away or those exquisite earrings that you have and put those on. NOW, how do you feel? Ready to take on the world!

It is amazing what clothes can do to a person's mental feeling. As you undress and put back on your stay-at-home clothes, what is the first thing you want to do? Sit down and watch TV. Notice that the feeling of "let's go do something!" instantly goes away? Your mind suddenly feels tired and lazy. Just think about that the next time you want to go out and impress someone: a prospect, a client, a date, a professional, etc. What do you want to feel like when you are about to represent your business, your name and your brand?

How Do You ACT?

How you feel directly affects how you act. When you are feeling down, you instantly want to crawl up and lie in bed. Contrastingly, when you are feeling great, you can't wait to go out and do something! You will also find that when you are feeling positive you start noticing more positive things and will do more positive things. You will smile more, be more friendly and more helpful. Subconsciously, you will pay attention to details more. You indirectly will take actions that will build upon the feeling that you have or to prevent the positive feeling from being tarnished.

Let's go back to the previous demonstration. Gals, as you were feeling awesome with your smart outfit and accessories, what did you do with your hands? And hair? That's right you flicked it or put it up or just simply tidied up a little. And guys, what did you do with your tie? You straightened it or retied it or changed it entirely. Why? Well you already felt great, but the fact that the tie is not exactly centered made you fix it. You wanted your hair to be perfect. You will notice the little bit of dust on your shoes, the wrinkle in your tie or the out of place strand of hair. Instantly, you would dust off your shoes, iron out your tie and comb that hair back in place. But none of that mattered when you didn't have on the outfit. The fact that the back piece of your tie is longer than the front piece and will be covered by your buttoned up jacket didn't matter. It had to be retied. We would do things to maintain the feeling of success. We would walk quicker yet more careful. Stand taller but relaxed. Adjust our clothes before sitting. You would be surprised that just the simple action of walking at a faster pace will lead you to more opportunities and success. Successful people have places to go and things to do and this is recognized by others. All of these actions and more are done to maintain that feeling of success.

As your attention to detail increases, you will find that your confidence rises. As your feelings feed your actions and your actions feed your feelings, you now know that you are confident and more motivated than ever to succeed.

What People Seeing You Will THINK

Now that you are feeling 12 out of 10, presenting yourself with success and professionalism, envision yourself as the person you are looking to impress. If you were a potential client, partner or date how would you feel about you? What would be your first impression be of yourself? You will find that you are your own biggest critic. Chances are good that you have picked out all your faults and fixed them before your prospect can find one.

What do you look for when you are looking for a partner? How do you feel when you see someone new? What gets you feeling – *'that is someone I want to talk to or get to know more'*? By putting yourself in the shoes of your potential clients and partners, you will be able to analyze yourself from a third party's point of view. You will automatically know whether what you are wearing impresses or does not impress. Whether your actions increase your likeability or decrease it.

Think back to our demonstration. If you were to hire you for a job, who would you hire? The version in your stay at home clothes? The version with a T-shirt and suit? Or the version with the make shift pocket chief? More importantly who would you ask to see first, the one in the flip flops or the one with the elegant earrings? In the end, what increases your chances of being talked to first? You may be the best at what you do or the best fit for that person, but if you do not show that you are worth getting to know, then you will forever be the diamond in the rough.

Act Like You Belong

Acting like you belong, like dressing like you belong, goes a long way as well. If you want to be successful you must act and think like successful people do. If you hang around people who complain a lot, you will eventually become a person who complains a lot. By putting yourself in situations where the people around you are successful or are people that you want to be, you will eventually start acting like those you want to be. You will notice that you start talking the same language, moving the same and dressing the same! For example, when you go to a club event of high net worth people, don't go in and feel like you are in the wrong place, go in thinking and feeling like you belong! Walk up to people and greet them like you know them. A great tip, is to call them by name. Chances are great, that they will have on name tags. When they hear their own name, they will feel like you belong. Note that the most beautiful sound for everyone is the sound of someone saying their name. You will be shocked at the difference in attitude if you just addressed people by their name. When going to a table, look as if you know exactly where it is. By doing so, regulars would feel that you are right there with them and that they just need to get to know you.

Figuring out how certain systems work also will allow you to learn how to act a certain way depending on what outcome you would like. An everyday errand like going to the bank has a lot more in play than one would think. If you would like to get a loan, don't just go to any bank and ask for a loan. Go to a few banks and just watch how things are done. See who walks in there, how people leave, who the tellers deal with and who comes from the offices. Watch how they dress and how they act. If you want to deal with people at the bank you must be like the people at the bank. Funny thing about banks is that they are happy to lend money when you don't need it. Getting a loan is hard when you need the money. So, what do you do? Get a loan when you don't need it. Have it all done and ready to go so that when you do need it, it's there. If you do need it, act like you don't. Act like you are there to do business, build a rapport with the people there and build friendships (to be discussed later). If you really look at the numbers, with respect to the loan at their interest, they should be running to you for your business. So act like you belong and see what a difference it will be next time you go to a bank.

Simply acting like you belong and dressing professionally makes a world of difference. Get a fresh haircut, get a suit, wear a power tie and shine your shoes. You will find that you stand taller and feel more confident. If you are still not convinced that by doing so, you will be approached with more opportunities to succeed - then we have one more demonstration.

Get two books: a dictionary and your favorite novel. Get a black sheet of paper and wrap the cover of the novel. Likewise get a red piece of paper and wrap the cover of the dictionary and in big black block letters write "READ ME, I WILL CHANGE YOUR LIFE!" on the front. Place these two books on your coffee table. Next time you have guests over keep tabs on which book is picked up first and opened. It is true that you should never judge a book by its cover, but without the cover, the book will never get a chance to be judged.

What to Wear

MALES:

- Black clean and pressed suit
    - o pays to invest in a couple of high-quality suits
- Power tie: solid eye catching colors
    - o gold, red, blue are highly recommended
- Black leather shoes – shined
- White shirt – this forces the tie to "pop!"
    - o colored shirts and patterned shirts must match the tie and should be worn after the first or second meeting of your potential target
- Matching pocket-chief with your tie
    - o a white pocket chief will work with all colors
- Dress socks – black or if colored, match with tie
- Belt with a clean sharp belt buckle
- Your most prized watch if it goes with the suit
- Cufflinks, if you have them
- A good pen – not your everyday BIC pens
- Make sure your hair is clean cut
- Leather wallet that matches the suit

FEMALES:

- Dress suit
- Pants suit
- Dress
- Blouse
- Jacket
- Closed-toed pumps

- Shoe color should coordinate with your purse color
- Shoes should be polished and clean – leather
- Skirt – comfortable and long enough to cover thigh when sitting
- Slit in skirt should be small and centered in the back

What to stay away from:

- Poor quality outfits
- Pattern extremes
- Wrinkles or uncomfortable materials like rayon and polyester that are warm
- Outfits that are too tight
- Chunky heels, flat soled-shoes, stilettos or extremely high heels

To be successful you must:
Look, Act and FEEL successful!

Chapter 2 – Dress for Success
Act Like You Belong

I had no idea of the character. But the moment I was dressed, the clothes and the make-up made me feel the person he was. I began to know him, and by the time I walked onto the stage, he was fully born.

- Charlie Chaplin -

Assurance Keys to Your Success

-   Dress to feel confident and comfortable

-   How you feel will feed how you act

-   How you act will feed how you feel

-   Attention to detail

-   Envision yourself as the person you are meeting

-   Treat your business like a business

-   Walk tall and at a faster pace

-   Stand tall and be confident and get noticed

-   Who you want to be is who you spend time with

-   Learn the system and culture of who you want to be

45

Chapter - 3 -

Networking:

Focus on Relationships

**It's not what you know or who you know,
It's who knows you.**

- J.T. Foxx -

*"We are pumped! We have our power ties and sharp
suits! We feel the part and are ready to act the part. But
where do we go? And most importantly what do we say
and do when we do meet people? We have no
experience in public speaking and have been really shy.
What do you recommend we do when it comes to
networking?" asked Melissa. Networking is one of the
most important keys to having a successful business.
Shyness can be overcome by action and networking
techniques.*

The most common questions with networking are: Where and How? Focus on relationships. People do business and invest with people they like and trust. Why do you buy certain items knowing that something out there is better? You did so because you felt a bond or relationship with the salesperson. We are no longer in the era where people need to be sold. Everyone is ready to buy. They already have educated themselves about certain products before they go looking for it. With all the information on the Internet, we are all able to compare, check prices and read reviews. What they don't expect is someone who is there to add value to their purchase or to enhance their buying experience. It is those salespeople who customers go back to and request their services. Why? It is the relationship that has been built one transaction at a time. It is these relationships that will ultimately help you Make More and Work Less.

Three keys to successful networking are:

- Key No. 1 - LISTEN more than talk
- Key No. 2 - How VALUE can be added
- Key No. 3 - NEVER sell

LISTEN more than talk

Have you ever noticed that when you are with people who like to talk and after an evening with them they say that they enjoyed the evening a lot and that it was great talking to you even if they did all the talking? Humans by nature like the sound of their own voice. When you genuinely express interest in what someone has to say you would be surprised how much they want to tell you. This is why we were given two ears and one mouth. So that we listen twice as much as we speak. By nature we are fearful of silence. If no one is talking, everyone will develop an urge to want to say something and get a conversation going again. Topics such as families, hobbies, vacation and work always are great conversation pieces. Not only do you get to learn more about certain topics that you may have never thought of, but you also will learn a lot more about the person and build a relationship. Having an engineering background, most of the people around us talk about construction, oil and gas, steel etc. never in our right minds would we have thought we'd meet a crime scene clean up expert, a professional Mixed Martial Arts fighter or a former Snow White at Disneyland! The stories that they shared and what we have learned about their occupation further allowed us to have a wider range of topics for us to discuss and stories to share. Before long, you will find that you have something to add with any topic as you will be able to connect to different industries and stories that you've heard before with new people that you are meeting.

How VALUE can be Added

As you are listening to the other person, you also must keep something very important in mind. The Golden Key to building relationships is: "How can I add value to this person?" People today are so busy thinking about themselves that it is very rare that someone else would have their best interest in mind. Not only are you listening intently to what they are saying but also have their best interest in mind. If you have this question in mind, you will start to look for areas where you can add value. Whether it's someone you can introduce to them who will solve their problem, or if it is something that you have that can assist them, or information that you know that can save them time, looking for opportunities to add value will be a great step in building a relationship. Our minds are set to reciprocate what we receive. If you were to add value to someone, chances are great, the favor will be returned and usually in much greater ways than you would have thought. If you were going into a conversation with someone who you know could help you with something, it is always better for them to suggest their assistance than to have you ask for it. But how can this happen? By adding value, what can you do to make things easier for them? What can you provide that would make them feel special? The return may not come immediately or at all, but when it does you can be assured that a great relationship may be in the making.

Recently, our real estate agent has offered to list a few of our properties and sell them for no fee! This was a complete surprise to us. We never would have thought that we could get a deal like that. Getting a couple of percentage points off, we could see, but for free? We were taken aback. Even so, we have agreed to offer him a fee for his services as we also value the time and effort that he will be putting into the sales. The point is that before he offered, we have never asked about discounts or special rates. What we have been doing is, connecting him to our network of investors and team members (as discussed before), shared information, material and recommending him to others. Once you realize that there are a lot more things that one can offer besides money, the more creative ways you'll be able to see to add value to others.

Another example of adding value is how we treat our tenants. That will be discussed later in this book. By putting ourselves in the shoes of our tenants, we were able to think of ways to add value to their moving in experience, which, in turn, led them to sending us referrals. Due to all the value we provide our tenants, they want their friends and family to have the same treatment and therefore will recommend us to help them.

NEVER sell

Networking key No. 3 is never ever sell to the person. The last thing you want to do is to have a potential client or partner label you as a "used car salesman". We all have this person in mind: someone who is only pushing for the sale, hiding the truth on certain items, not genuine, constantly talking about how great they are and why you need to buy. If those are the people that you stay away from, then those are the people that you definitely do not want to become. The fact is, as long as you follow the first two Keys: *Listen* intently and look to *Add Value* you will automatically not sell. You will find that you will answer questions and add information about what you do and know when prompted. The person genuinely wants to hear more about what you have to say.

Always remember to read the listener. Look at their body language: are they checking their watch? Are they eyeing the door? Are they leaning forward? Are they responding to your information positively?

Listen to their responses: Are they replying with skepticism, or with excitement? Are they yawning or speaking very slowly? All these are clues as to whether the information you are telling them is adding value or not. As long as you pay attention to your listener, you will find that avoiding the dreaded "used car salesman" stereotype is very natural.

Where Do We Go?

This is all nice and dandy. We now know what to do but where do we find people? There are numerous places and opportunities in which you can network. Everywhere you see people is a networking opportunity. Depending on what you are looking for will determine where you need to be. Think about what your target audience likes to do or go? Go to those places. Of course that is not to say you couldn't find or meet your target listener at the local grocery market, but you would like to increase your chances to meet your ideal audience more efficiently. There are four groups of places where you can network depending on who you want to meet:

- Group No. 1
  - o Everyday places, bank, bus stop, elevator, work, etc.

- Group No. 2
  - o Courses/seminars/events/clubs of what you are doing

- Group No. 3
  - o Courses/seminars/events/clubs of different industries

- Group No. 4
  - o Charity functions, political gatherings

- Group No. 5
  - o Bonus Locations!

After discussing the first four groups, we will then reveal two groups where education and networking will go hand in hand.

Group 1 - Everyday Places

Everyday locations can be networking gems. Ever get into the situation where you are in an elevator and everyone in the elevator presses themselves against the walls and looks forward or at the ground? At all costs, they are trying desperately not to make eye contact with each other. Why is that? Why are we all so afraid to get to know people and meet new friends? You never know, that person in the corner of the elevator could be a potential partner or client. Think of all the exciting stories that you have in your life. Where you have been, what you do, surprises that you have experienced. They too have lives and stories just as exciting as yours! People in general are very talkative people, by nature we are all just afraid of "breaking the ice" and starting the conversation. Look at these situations as learning experiences. Next time you walk into an elevator, approach the next person you see and ask how their day is going. If you are at a restaurant, get to know the people around you and ask if they come to this place often. Or ask the person beside you at a theater before the movie starts, what they have heard about the movie or why they decided to see it that night. Of course, you will need to be able to read the body language of the person to see if you are actually engaging them into a conversation or annoying them. There is a very fine line between developing a relationship versus becoming a pest.

Get to know the people you work with, what their hobbies are and what their vacation plans are. Before long, the people at work may become those who will partner up with you in the end. At the very least, you will begin to realize that working with those people become easier and easier. Things become less robotic and more fun. Co-workers will become more willing to help you and vice versa. That person that you see at the bus stop everyday will no longer be "that person" but will soon have a name, a life and an existence in yours.

Next time you are at a bank, find out what the person in front of you in the line does for a living. You already have something in common with them, you chose the same bank! This usually means that they either live or work near-by, another thing that you have in common! These everyday situations also will have the widest variety of people that you will meet. These are people with experiences unlike your own and when a relationship is built you will learn a lot about their interests, line of work and in general - people. The fact is there is a chance you may never see these people again but if there is a connection, the sky's the limit. Use these opportunities to hone your skills: listen and visualize how you can add value. You will find that these instances will help you later in other networking situations.

Group 2 - Where You Go to Increase Your Skills

Now it is true that these everyday situations may not present you with the people that can help you with what you want to accomplish, but it's a good place to start. To meet those that are similar to your mindset and looking for the same things you are looking for, just think of locations that you can go to improve yourself. These are the locations where you will find people who may help you along the way with what you are going to accomplish. These also are the places where you may find pieces to your team (to be discussed in the next chapter).

To stay with the context of this book we will use the real estate investor's environment. As real estate investors, it is very important to understand that you cannot do everything yourself. There is no way for you to do every deal out there and that there are plenty of deals. So get to know who is out there doing what you are doing and find ways of adding value to them. You will realize that even though you are all doing the same thing, we all have pieces of the puzzle missing. We all have weaknesses and strengths. The largest advantage with networking in these locations is that you all "speak" the same language and that you can actually help each other. One may have a property to sell and you may have the right buyer for that property. One may have a property that is best for a certain exit strategy that they don't know about but you do. These also are the best places to collaborate and bounce ideas. Discuss about what is working and what is giving you a challenge. You would be surprised how many people have the same challenges that you have and yet be ever so willing to share how they were able to overcome it. As they say:

"A wise man learns from his mistakes while a genius learns from other people's mistakes."

So where do these people connect? For real estate, there are numerous local clubs and groups that meet up monthly or even weekly where the main reason is to bounce ideas and learn from each other. These groups will usually bring in speakers on topics that will help you with your ventures whether it's a property manager talking about finding tenants or a mortgage broker sharing the best rates and lenders, there is always something to learn at these get-togethers.

Similarly, sign up for courses, events and seminars that are there to teach about certain topics regarding real estate. For instance: a two-day course on Lease Options, a three-hour evening seminar on how to do tax liens, or a five-day event where experts and professionals talk about how they became successful. These are the places where everyone like you, are looking to: sharpen their tools, learn more about the industry and are all looking for people like you to work together toward a common goal. You will find that networking with these people is very easy, because you will have a lot in common. However, remember to listen, think of how to add value and do not sell until prompted. By remembering these three keys you will be set aside from everyone else. This is because everyone else is busy telling everyone else what they have to offer without listening to the other people. They go on and on about their projects and their deals, that they forget that not all deals fit all investors. When you come up and you genuinely listen and ask questions about their day-to-day lives, what you are getting them to talk about is a breath of fresh air compared to all the talk about real estate. By networking and learning about their lives, you will have begun a relationship with that person that may lead to deals and partnerships. This will never happen if you are focused on selling the listener about your opportunity when you first met them.

Group 3 - Where Other People in Other industries Go to Increase Their Skills

You now know that just within the real estate investor's environment, there are numerous courses, seminars, clubs, events and groups that you can attend or join. It is only logical that within each industry, be it teachers, doctors, car salesman, home entertainment systems, etc., they also have gatherings of clubs and events. Seminars and courses for hobbyist and fans of sports are very popular. Conventions for those who love fishing and courses on how to make a better omelet, happen every day throughout the year. Why, you ask, are we interested in a class about photography or dinner seminars about the latest news in the oil and gas industry for engineers? It is at these events and gatherings that you can start learning how best to "get through" to them, how to speak their language and how to get them to remember you when the time comes for them to inquire about real estate investing. As an investor, there comes a point in time where you will run out of your own capital, but great deals and opportunities will continue to come your way. It is at this time that a joint venture partner or a money partner would be best to have in your back pocket. Professionals have a passion for their trade, whether it is helping people with their health or designing bridges for a city, professionals love what they do and are usually in a pretty good financial situation. Teachers have a great connection to the community and what families want for their children. They are very involved with people within the community.

Depending on what you seek to get out of it will determine which group you would like to know better if not all of them. For example, if you were looking for a money partner and you know of a seminar where engineers gather, find out what is needed to attend that seminar. When asked why you are there tell them the truth, that you have a fascination about the industry and would like to learn more about it. You will realize that, of the entire room, you are the only expert in your field of real estate investing. As you get to know the people in this group, you will understand what they want in investing, why they don't and why what they are doing is not working. Knowing the solutions to their problems, you will become the "expert" that they will now go to when it comes to advice or suggestions about investing. Before long, you will have a list of interested potential money partners that you'd be able to pass your projects to for their thoughts. Never sell them on the project, present it to them and ask for their thoughts or ask whether or not you should proceed with the project. By asking them about their thoughts, if the project is of value, they will not feel like being sold to, would be honored that you asked them for their thoughts and may in fact be interested themselves. Therefore, without 'selling' them on your project, they voluntarily will want you to tell them more about it. Note that this will only work with some people. Others will want you to be the expert and not ask for their advice.

Likewise, if you wanted to know more about a certain area due to properties that are available you could consider attending community events or parent-teacher groups. When asked why you are there, again tell them the truth and say that you are interested in the area as a potential place to live. Again, meeting the people in this group will allow you to understand the pros and cons of the area, which areas to avoid, such as areas with high traffic. You may meet the neighbors of a potential property that's available. People like to talk about what is happening where they are living so you will be able to learn a lot about a certain area. Similarly, like at the engineering dinner event, you will find that you can possibly be the only person in the room working in real estate, where others will deem you as the expert. People generally like to invest in their own back yard and sometimes even in their own community. Therefore, you may have potential joint venture partners in the room wanting to know more about what you do.

Group 4 - Where Successful People Go

Courses, seminars, events and conventions are great to meet people from all different forms of work but where can one find the "blue chip" money partners? Those who can, if the relationship is built right, become a money partner for life. These are the partners who can help you buy properties with cash, allowing you to close deals faster. These are the relationships that will be there when you need cash fast to secure a multi-unit deal.

People of this caliber, who may be in the gatherings that we mentioned before, usually run with another crowd. It is said that:

"Tell me who your closest five friends are, and I'll tell you who you are, tell me the average income of your five closest friends and I can tell you what you make."

Successful people spend time with successful people. If anything, to be associated with a group of successful people, you too will learn to be successful.

By networking and building relationships with successful people, you will find that you will subconsciously build yourself up to be at the level they are. If they are at a 10 and you are at a six, you will eventually become an eight. A story that comes to mind is about an investor.

Jack deems himself as a real estate investor because he has a rental property that is cashflowing well for the last five years. From that moment, he has not added any new properties. His friend Bob, an active real estate investor, invited Jack into a mastermind group that he attends with other successful real estate investors. At the start of each meeting, they go around the table and introduce themselves and what they have done during the past month. One said that he just picked up two properties and is renovating another. Another one says that she had a slow month and only did two wholesale deals and on it went. When it came to Jack, he said he is managing a rental property that he bought five years ago. The next month, the same thing happened. People talked about what they did to increase their portfolio and here Jack was managing his property. Feeling behind, Jack worked hard the following month because he was getting tired of telling people that he was just managing one property. By the next meeting, due to the hard work, the determination and the will to want to belong, Jack was able to announce that he purchased another property.

Spending time with people more successful than you is a great way to improve on what you are doing. You get a sense of self-motivation to want to do more. Hearing other success stories will encourage you to want to have one yourself. As the great Nido Qubein says:

"If you want to be rich, do what rich people do. If you don't want to be poor, watch what poor people do and don't do it. If you are spending most of your time with a bunch of dingalings, then you are a dingaling in the making!"

So where do these successful people like to gather? Political rallies, fundraisers, charities, dinner galas and elite clubs. When it comes to dinner galas and elite clubs, getting the opportunity to attend these does not come often or easily, these will come though and when they do, remember to act like you belong. Political rallies, fundraisers and charity functions however, are often open to everyone. Volunteering to help out your party in an upcoming election will open doors to networking with high caliber personnel. Attending a charity function and donating will not only show that you care about the community, but also get you noticed by others with great influences in the community. During these gatherings, be sure not to sell or promote your business. It is all about the rally or the charity. Focus on why the charity is important and reason for having the gathering, talking about business can happen at a later date when you have built a rapport with whom you are networking with.

You will find that successful people know other successful people. If you have built the relationship with a few successful people, by adding value to them as discussed before, you may be invited to such dinner galas or clubs where you will meet more potential partners. Remember to focus on what they are looking for and what you can do to add value to them. Do not flat out ask them what they want, do your research. If you know which certain people will be at the functions or charities, find out more about them. Ask people at the event if they know anything about that person or search online to see what they have done. The more you know about the person, the more equipped you are when it comes time for you to talk to them. People of success's highest commodity is time, you do not want to waste their time. If you can show that you respect and value their time, they will notice that you are a little different than a lot of other people that approach them. By doing your research, you will also find out how you can add value to that person. It may be someone you know from your other networking events that you can connect them to or you may have a perfect opportunity for them, it is at this time that you can stand out further in their minds by adding value to them. Once you have established that and have built a relationship, these are the people that will become a great asset in the future.

Group 5 - SHY?...Pah! Bonus places for great networking

Well, yes all this networking is great, but what if you are shy and not very good at speaking you ask. Funny that you should mentioned that. When we first started getting into investing in real estate, we knew that networking is not our strong suit. We were the type that would sit somewhere in the middle to back, stand off to the side or outright too afraid to go to an event. Even if attending courses and rallies etc. forced us from our comfort zone, we knew we had to do more to improve our public speaking skills. This is when we discovered two great organizations that not only helped with our speaking abilities but also provided great networking and relationship building opportunities: Toastmasters and Dale Carnegie.

Toastmasters

Toastmasters is not a club that sits around talking about toasters and how to make breakfast. Toastmasters is a club in which you can join for a minimal fee where people are all there for the same thing you are: improving their abilities to speak, have confidence in crowds and becoming leaders. Within the club, there are different speaking roles that allow you to, at your own pace, develop and build on your confidence and speaking ability. From giving reports about meetings to telling a joke, to running a meeting and to present a speech, Toastmasters is a great place for you to learn how to speak in front of others and develop leadership skills. Not only do you get practice preparing presentations and formal speeches, but you also get to hone your "quickness on your feet" skill as impromptu speaking is another side of Toastmasters that is available. Since Toastmasters is open to all who are interested, you also will meet a wide variety of people of different industries looking to learn. You will find that you will get to build relationships with fellow toastmasters.

Dale Carnegie

Dale Carnegie is another great location to develop great speaking skills. Their introductory course focuses on human relations. During the course, you will learn about how people react and think and ultimately how to build strong relationships. During each class, you will be asked to get up in front of the class and through personal stories demonstrate how you applied the teachings of human relations. You will start to develop a method of speaking in which you can use stories to get your point through to potential clients. People love stories and tend to live through other peoples experiences. Have you noticed how sports fans relive the moment of an outstanding play? They weren't even the ones scoring that goal or making the basket, but they are able to retell the play to its smallest details as if they were the one making the shot. Story telling is one of the most effective ways of communicating ideas and thoughts. The beautiful part of this is that the story is yours. You know the story and therefore, when you tell it, it sounds exciting as you are reliving the moment. The story also will be authentic and true. It is not memorized or written, but it is from the heart. You will find by telling stories while you network, networking becomes a lot more natural because you are confident with what you have to say. Again, like Toastmasters, Dale Carnegie is open to everyone of all industries, creating a great environment for you to network and build relationships.

There will come a time where you would like someone to connect you with people that they know. Once you have gotten to the point in the relationship where you have shown that you are a valuable asset in their lives, having them make the connection with someone they know can help you will be easy. A very important tip to remember is this:

"NEVER EVER ask for a referral, Ask for an introduction."

When people ask for referrals, the person being asked is now feeling an obligation to do it for you, to find the referral, it becomes work to them. Therefore, a referral is only effective three of 10 times. However, when you are asking for an introduction with someone, people are genuinely happy to do so. They are proud to be associated with your project and the person they know. The words "introduction' and "referral" over time have generated completely different feelings. The word 'referral' has a generally negative connotation where everything feels money-based. On the other hand, the word 'introduction' has more of a positive feeling and more relationship-based. When asked for an introduction, eight of 10 times, you will be successful.

How to Find and Sign up

Of course, there are many different groups and courses and events out there. The best way to find them is to search online or ask friends and people that you met who are good at something you would like to know. Business Network International and Meetup Groups are two other great places to build a group around for networking. If dressing for success is an important first step in achieving your goals in becoming an investor, then putting yourself out there in different groups is a very close second. Not only will you meet many interesting people and build great relationships, but you also will build your knowledge about different aspects and industries in life allowing you to be more versatile. As long as you remember the three keys of networking: Listen, Add Value and Never Sell, you will make a great impression in any group setting and surround yourself with people that will help you Make More and Work Less with Cashflow.

For great events to attend, JT Foxx has many events throughout the world that is great for networking, opportunities and learning great content. Author of *Business Lessons from JT Foxx*, we have been very fortunate to have met JT Foxx and applied many of his teachings. If not for him we would not be where we are today.

We can all work together to provide the missing pieces!

Chapter 3 – Networking: Focus on Relationships

Successful people are always looking for opportunities to help others. Unsuccessful people are always asking, "What's in it for me?"

- Brian Tracy -

Assurance Keys Your Success

- LISTEN more than talk

- ADD VALUE

- *NEVER sell*

- Everyday networking locations

- Courses/events/seminars of your industry

- Courses/events/seminars of other industries

- Focus on charities and political party's goals

- Toastmasters and Dale Carnegie will help with shyness and networking

- Who you spend time with is who you will become

- Never ask for a referral, ask for an introduction

- Look for places to get involved

Chapter - 4 -

Power Teams

Do it All

**Talent wins games, but teamwork
and intelligence wins championships.**

- Michael Jordan -

Shortly after our conversation about networking, John texted us and asked: "There is so much stuff that we don't know. From contracts to finances to renovation materials, how can one do all that stuff?" To that we told John: "Exactly. You can't do it all yourself and that is why you need a Super TEAM of individuals to help you along the way. We'll get together and we'll show you how to construct a dream TEAM!"

MAKE MORE WORK LESS with CASHFLOW

Just as a superstar athlete needs a team to win the game, you will need a team to help you do all the things needed in acquiring cashflowing properties. We call this a power team.

There are many people that make up a power team. A power team member is available for each task of acquiring cashflowing properties, from finding properties to closing on them. Not only do you need to know what role they play, but you also will need to know where to find them. Once you have a great team, the quest to Make More and Work Less with Cashflow becomes more of a reality.

Real Estate Agent

A real estate agent can help you find properties that could meet your requirements. You will need to inform him or her about the properties you seek. A real estate agent can easily help you set up a search on multiple listing services to target the properties that meet your criteria.

Real estate agents also can help set up showings at the properties you deem to have potential as cashflowing properties. When you find a property you like and before you see it, you will want to ask your real estate agent to get you a comparable market analysis. A CMA is something that a real estate agent can do to determine what the property you want is worth. They do this by comparing the property to other properties that are listed or were sold in the area. Keep in mind that a CMA is an art and not a science. You will need to look at the CMA and determine if the other properties are truly comparable to the one you are considering. Sometimes, what a real estate agent will do, especially those unfamiliar or new to this is that they take properties that have the same number of bedrooms, but, in an area of town just far enough to have a different environment. For those more familiar with the market, they will know that sometimes just a few streets will make a lot of difference in price point of a property. If you are unsure of the CMA your real estate agent provided, you may want to consider looking for a second opinion. If the second opinion is very different, what you can do is ask both real estate agents to validate the CMA they have provided.

Most real estate agents work with the MLS only, but some real estate agents also can sometimes find deals for you before they are listed. These deals are primed for you because no one else knows about them yet. However, be aware that these are not always the best deals. You must still do your due diligence prior to putting in an offer on a property.

Questions for your Real Estate Agent:

Do you invest yourself?
Do you work with investors?
Do you have experience dealing with investors?
What are your specialties?
Where are you most successful?
What types of properties do you deal with most?

The answers to these questions will allow you to determine if he or she is the real estate agent for you. For instance, if they are not investors themselves then they may not understand why you offer the numbers you offer and why you can't close on certain deals. If agents are investors and have experience with investors, then they will understand why you do what you do and will be a better asset to you. Working to the strengths of your real estate agent may prove to be very beneficial. If they are experts in basement-suited homes, then chances are great they have seen many of these properties and will be able to give powerful insight and find the best deals for you. The goal here is to eventually have your real estate agent find you the deals so that you don't have to search for them. The more your real estate agent understands what your goals are, the more he or she can help you.

Mortgage Broker

A mortgage broker is the person you would need when you want to finance a property and have no investor lined up to do so. A mortgage broker is much like those that you find in a major bank. The difference is that they have access to many lenders, rather than just one bank. The key part to this is when shopping for a mortgage, every bank you check, will pull your credit. When you check enough banks that pull your credit, your credit rating will drop. A mortgage broker differs in that they only need to pull your credit once and they can use it for multiple lenders at the same time without hurting your credit.

You don't have to pay for a mortgage broker as the lenders pay them when you get a mortgage with them. This is where you must be careful. Some mortgage brokers will match you up with a lender where they will get the most benefit. These are not the mortgage brokers you want. The mortgage broker that you want to find is one that will get you a mortgage based on your needs, not theirs.

Once you find the right mortgage broker for you, you will find that the financing world will become much easier. They are the experts in mortgages, and with lenders changing the rules so often, they are your best source of information when it comes to lending.

Questions for your Mortgage Broker:

Do you work with investors?
Do you invest yourself?
Are you creative in finding lenders?
Do you have access to private lenders?
Do you have experience working with investors who have multiple properties?
What hours do you work?

Similar to the real estate agent, the answer to these questions are very important. Some brokers are used to working one deal at a time and don't usually have repeat customers. Others do not have access to certain mortgage products that will suit your needs. You are looking for a broker that is experienced and will help you find the best product available. You're looking for someone that you can strategize a plan as to how you can accumulate multiple properties. A great broker will also be there for you on the weekends and after hours. When it comes to closing deals and getting financing, it is in your best interest to have a broker who is willing to work after hours to secure you the products that you need.

Title Company

Once you build a relationship with a mortgage broker, you will want to find a title company that will work with both your real estate agent and your mortgage broker. Title companies are valuable to make the closing go smoothly. They ensure the properties you are considering are without liens or problems when acquiring. They also can alert you to possible problems with certain types of closing settlements. This will save you time in the long run. Often, title companies have lawyers on staff that will help you with the paperwork. It is common that your lawyer will take care of the title company and all paperwork associated as well.

Contractor

Contractors can help you with assessing what needs to be fixed and how much it will cost. When you are first looking for them, ask for a quote from several contractors to see what they say. Sometimes, you will find that the quotes are very different. This is when it becomes important to look at what they are specifically quoting. There are some contractors that will try to fix everything. That will be perfect if you were living in the house, but with cashflowing properties, it needs to make sense. For example, if the roof still has about two years left before it is anticipated to be changed, then why not wait a bit while you increase your cash from the rental before you replace the roof? We are by no means saying that you should cut corners, we are merely saying that you need to assess what is important to be fixed right now. Anything that could pose a safety concern must be fixed prior to having someone move into it. Otherwise, you will be faced with very serious issues.

Good contractors become a great asset for you. If the relationship is built, they can provide you with great insight as to how much things will cost to fix. There may be opportunities where you need to bring them in for a viewing so that you can put in a reasonable offer. Having a reliable and trustworthy contractor also gives you the peace of mind that if anything goes wrong with any of your properties that you will always have someone you trust to fix the problem.

If your contractors are interested, there is always the possibility of them becoming a joint venture partner on a property with you. They provide the materials and renovations and you provide the expertise and financing to secure a cashflow property.

Questions for your Contractor:

What trades do you know?
Do you have any references?
Do you have pictures of past work?
Are you an investor?
How long would it take you to do a full-house renovation?
Do you have a team to help you?

Property Inspector

Property inspectors will help you inspect the house for things that may need to be replaced or replaced soon. They will inspect things like the furnace, hot water tank, roof (if it is safe to inspect), foundation and so on. They can even inspect and advise if they think there is asbestos in the property. While they are not allowed to move anything, they will certainly inspect everything they can. An inspection cannot protect you from everything, but it will give you a good idea of what you can expect prior to buying the property.

Good property inspectors will have many years of experience and have references to share. They also will prepare detailed reports and can do the inspections within three to four hours for an average single family home. Property inspectors who are open to showing you what they do and how they do it are most advantageous. These are the inspectors who will allow you to follow them around to watch what they do and ask them questions. Following a good inspector around will allow you to learn the trade and save you from unexpected problems if you know what to seek.

Property Manager

A property manager can help you in maintaining the property after you have purchased it. We strongly encourage you to do this yourself at the beginning to learn how it works, but as you keep acquiring more properties, you will find that it helps to have someone manage the properties for you. A property manager should be able to do everything for you from advertising for tenants, doing a background and credit check on them and dealing with any concerns with the tenants.

Good property managers are hard to find, which is why we suggest you learn how to do it yourself first. Once you get a good idea of what a property manager should do, you can work together to ensure that things are done the way you want it to be done. More information on managing properties can be found in Section 3.

Questions for your Property Manager:

Do you invest yourself?
Do you have a team to help you?
How do you find and screen your tenants?
How many doors do you manage?
How many years have you been managing properties?
Do you have references to share?
Will you go to court on my behalf if need be?
What are the most interesting/difficult properties that you have managed?

The experience of property managers can prove to be a great asset to you. They might have a property that is about to be sold, in which, they can contact you first. The better the property manager, the less headaches you will experience.

Lawyer

A lawyer will help you out with the legal matters of acquiring the property. This will include reviewing the offer, checking the title of the property to ensure that it is free and clear (this means that there are no liens on the property) and also the transferring of title to your name should you lift all conditions. Lawyers also can answer other real estate issues that might arise, including landlord-tenant issues. Property disputes also would be resolved with your lawyer. He or she can draft all your documents as we will discuss later.

Questions for your Lawyer:

Do you deal with Investors?
What is your experience with real estate?
Are you an investor yourself?
What are your average fees?
How do you structure real estate for best asset protection?
Do you specialize in real estate or business law?
Do you represent landlords?

Bookkeeper

A bookkeeper will help you keep your expenses and revenues in order. This will help you track your business better and put it in a way that your accountant can easily use. It will be to your best interest to have the bookkeeper work in unison with your accountant. This way, communications will be easier when the accountant needs something. It is not too important if the bookkeeper does not have investor experience.

Accountant

As you know, accountants can help you file your taxes. What you will find more helpful is their expert knowledge in how you can keep more of your money and pay less taxes. A good accountant will be able to help you assess your situation and advise if something should be done a certain way. It could be as simple as putting something in your personal name rather than your company name, to something more complex like paying shareholder dividends versus a salary.

An accountant with investor experience will be a great advantage. However, if they are not investors themselves, as long as they are working with you to find the best way of filing your taxes then it is sufficient. Similar to the lawyer, your accountant will need to have great experience in accounting to correctly record what it is you need for tax purposes. A great accountant will come to you and discuss better ways to plan future meetings, charity donations, flow of money to best maximize the money that stays in your hands.

Investor

An investor comes in handy when you don't have enough capital to do what you want. An investor can range from helping you qualify for a property to putting in the money required to acquire a property. We will discuss this more thoroughly in Section 3.

Coach

A coach is one of the most vital team members you can have. He or she should be someone who is currently doing what you want to do. If he or she has done it in the past and is not currently doing it, then be cautious that their information may not be relevant to the market today. The market is constantly changing and if you aren't currently in it, you will be out of date with how things are done. A coach is vital in that he or she can help you avoid the mistakes that they have made and guide you in a way to faster success, rather than having you stumbling around blind. Remember back in the chapter on mindset? As you are learning about cashflowing properties, there always will be things that you don't know. A coach can point potential issues out for you and show you how to mitigate them before they happen.

A coach also is able to show you where you can go. They can show you what may have been impossible in your mind and make it possible. Coaches should be experienced, accountable, motivational, inspirational and friends. They should have your best interest in mind. You should bounce all decisions about real estate with your real estate coach.

Just like athletes have a nutrition coach, a game coach, a mentality coach, a coach for technique, it is to your advantage to have multiple coaches for the multiple aspects of your life.

Build the Relationships

Remember that you only can get out of each team member what you put in there. Never expect that your team members will do everything for you. If you do not discuss and plan what you want and what your goals are, you are limiting what your team members can do for you. For instance, a coach is very similar to your doctor. If you always tell your doctor that everything is fine, but you are actually looking for a cure for your sore throat, your doctor wouldn't know that you were in pain. Similarly, if you don't share the problems that you are experiencing and are not asking the questions needed to help you reach your goals, then your coach wouldn't know how to help you.

Now that you know what role your team members will play, you need to know where to find them. We have found that the best way is through networking and asking for introductions as we have talked about in the previous chapter. If no one you know can connect you to a team member, then you will need to search on your own. The easiest way is to look on Google for local team members. When you find them, make sure you interview them to see if they have the same belief system as you. You must be able to find team members that would work well with you, people that you like and vice versa. To make the interview process easier, set a day where you will see three to four real estate agents in a row at the same location one after another. Likewise do the same with a group of mortgage brokers. This will allow you to make an assessment when all the interviews are fresh in your mind and easy to compare. Once you have found the real estate agent or mortgage broker that you like, chances are great they have members of your power team that they use. Always ask them to make an introduction and interview their recommendations as well.

Once you have found the team members you wish, you can start focusing on building the relationship. Keep in mind that if you find that your chosen team member is not as good as you thought, you can start the whole process again to find someone else more suitable for you.

We have found that the best way to build a relationship with your team members is to add value to them. What is most important to them? How can you help them? By focusing on them first, you will find that it will come back to you ten-fold. This all ties back to the previous chapter where we talked about adding value to others first. If you know of potential clients for your power team, always send them their way. You will be surprised to see how much impact you will have if you were to consistently send new clients to your mortgage broker, lawyer, real estate agent, etc.

A great power team is one where you all can benefit each other. In a sense, members of your power team may be your mastermind group. Not only should you build the relationship with the members of your power team but the members within the power team also should know each other. For example, your real estate agent and your mortgage broker are two people that will be doing a lot of communications with each other. It will be to your best interest that they work well together. If you have members that you trust, do not be afraid to share your contacts with them and work together. Remember, strong relationships will help each other succeed.

The most important thing to keep in mind with your team members is that no one is more important than another. Whether it is your contractor, lawyer or investor, each one plays a critical role in helping you acquire cashflowing properties. Imagine a building being supported by nine pillars. What happens if you take one away? The building's support will weaken right? The more pillars you remove, the weaker the building support gets until finally it collapses.

Just as a building's support is dependent on strong pillars, a strong team will help you to Make More and Work Less with Cashflow.

Success is the work of all those around you.
Together, you will be stronger than any one person.

Chapter 4 – Power Teams Do it All

If everyone is moving forward together, then success takes care of itself.

- Henry Ford -

Assurance Keys to Your Success

- Interview potential power team members

- Choose the team members that you feel will work best with you

- Real Estate Agent
- Mortgage Broker
- Title Company
- Contractor
- Property Manager
- Lawyer
- Bookkeeper
- Accountant
- Investor
- Coach

- Add value to your team members first

- Build the relationships with each member of your power team and also among each of them

- Strategize and plan with all your team members

- SECTION 2 -

Acquiring Properties

It is true that you should develop your mindset and your team before you take big steps into the world of real estate investing, but you will realize that, sometimes, the mindset and the team members will come as you take those steps. A great power team takes time to build and maintain and, likewise a proper mindset may take years to develop. However do not let the absence of a team member or the fear of taking action stop you. You will find that it all grows and fills together as you take action toward your goal to Make More and Work Less with Cashflow.

Chapter - 5 -

Know Your Market Part I:
Be Aware of What You Can Do

**Research is what I'm doing when
I don't know what I'm doing.**

- Wernher Von Braun -

After some time, our friends John and Melissa came back and said: "We got most of our power team together and have been networking at many different events. We're ready to pick up properties and really jump into things. What's the first thing we need to do?"

Now that you have developed the mindset and parts of your team, the fun begins. When you buy a car or a TV, you do research. You should do the same with an investment property. You also have to know what exit strategy you are going to choose to use. There are many types of properties such as: single family homes, duplexes, condos, multi-family etc., and, likewise, many different exit strategies.

The four main investing exit strategies are:

1. Wholesale – Short-Term Capital without owning
2. Rent to Own – Short/Long-Term Cashflow
3. Buy-Fix-Flip – Short-Term – Capital Generator
4. Buy-Hold – Long-Term Cashflow Opportunity

Wholesaling

Wholesaling properties is a method where you as the investor will never hold the property but only the contract. You then find a buyer for that property who you will then close with for a fee.

For example: Let's say you have agreed to terms with Jill to buy her property for $200,000, down from the initial asking price of $220,000 and have signed the contract. You know you have about 10 business days to secure a buyer for that property. From your list of buyers that are interested in this type of property which you have developed through networking, you found Paul who would like to buy the property. You and Paul then agree that he will buy the property from you for $205,000. At the date of possession of the house from Jill to you, you will close the deal with Jill and hours later, after you get the keys, close your deal with Paul. At the end of the day you have made $5,000 without ever taking possession of the property.

Wholesaling

Contract to sell to you   Contract to sell to Paul

Hold the Contract

JILL → YOU → PAUL

$200,000   **$5,000**   **$205,000**
                     Profit

Rent-to-Own

Rent to Owning a property works very similarly to leasing a car. With a property that you have bought, you will find a tenant buyer for the property. Tenant buyers who are interested in this scenario are usually those who are unable to purchase a property now, be it poor credit or lack of a down payment but would love to be a home owner. This is how you can help. After you have found the tenant buyer, you will be renting the property to them with the option to purchase the property after a specified term, usually three to five years. You will require a fee as an option consideration which will go toward their future down payment for the house. This amount is usually about three month's rent, which is not enough to cover the 5 percent minimum required to purchase the house in the future. Therefore, depending on the agreed term, the remainder of the required down payment will be spread out throughout the term through rent as credit toward the future down payment at the end of the term if they choose to exercise the option. During the life of the term, your property will cashflow more due to the extra rent credit and you also will ensure that your tenant buyer is set up to succeed in exercising the option to buy the property. This means that they will be in contact with your team members, such as the mortgage broker and credit counselor. When the term is up and your tenant buyer has fulfilled all requirements to qualify for the property and decides to exercise the option to buy the property, the property will be sold to them at the current market price. A down payment for the property is not required as the rent credits and the option consideration at the beginning of the term will have made up for at least the 5 percent down. If the tenant buyer decides to not buy the property, then they will forfeit the option consideration and the rent credit that was accumulated. The advantages of this strategy is that you will have positive cashflow throughout the term of the option, have tenants that will treat the property like their home and also have the buyer in place that will buy your property for the future price at the end of the term.

Rent-To-Own

Owner = You
Current Price = $200,000

Future Price = $220,000

Future Tenant Buyer
Down Payment Needed
=$11,000
Down Payment Now
= $3,600

Three-year term
Current Rent = $1,200
Rent Credit = $206/month
Total Rent + Credit = $1,406
Monthly Expense = $1,000
Total Cashflow = $406/month

End of term:
Tenant buyer buys property:
$220,000 – $3600 – (36 months X $206) = $209,000

You collected:
$14,616 from three years of Cashflow plus $9,000 at close

Net profit = $21,616 (after estimated lawyer fees of $2,000)

Buy-Fix-Flip

Buy-Fix-Flip is a strategy where you will purchase a run-down property, fix it up cosmetically and then put it back into the market for sale. This strategy requires you to find properties that need work and also have people who can do renovations for you or do it yourself. For example, say you found a property that needs a lot of work: new floors, new kitchen, bathroom, new paint, new electrical etc. Due to its' current condition you were able to pick it up for $150,000. You know that if it was all fixed up that you would be able to sell the property for $300,000. After accessing the amount of work that needs to be done, you were given a quote of $60,000 that would bring the value of your property to the estimated $300,000. After all the repairs and selling costs you will then profit $67,000 usually in a span of four to six months.

Buy-Fix-Flip

 →→ → 6 months

Current value = $150,000   Fixed up = $300,000
Renovation Cost = $60,000   Selling cost = $13,000
Lawyer fee = $2,000
Holding Cost = $8,000
(Cost for 6months, ex. mortgage, utilities, property tax and insurance)

Total = $220,000   Remaining = $287,000

Net Profit = $67,000

Buy-Hold

Buy and hold is where you purchase a property, fix it up if need be, rent it out and do so for five plus years, where every month throughout the years, you will be profiting after all the expenses of maintaining the property is paid. After five years, you can decide to keep holding the property or sell it. For the purposes of this book, we will go into depth as to how to find, purchase, rent and maintain a Buy and Hold property, otherwise known as a Cashflow property. Also for the purposes of this book, we will be focusing on the single family homes that allow for separate basement suites. Those are the easiest buy-and-hold properties that an investor can get.

Buy-Hold

Expenses: Mortgage and Interest = $850/month
Property Tax = $150/month
Insurance = $50/month

Income: Main Rent = $1,100
Basement Rent = $850

Total Cashflow per month = $900

Total Cashflow after five years = $54,000

Set Up a Search

Now that we know what we want, we need to understand what the market is like for that type of property. This is where your real estate agent will play a great role. If you have chosen your real estate agents well, they should know where the best rental properties are and which locations are hot markets. Ask your real estate agent to set up a search for all single family homes, with the potential to or currently have:

- Basement suite
- Separate entrances
- Two to three bedrooms upstairs
- One to two bedrooms downstairs
- One to two bathrooms upstairs
- One bathroom down

Now with the expertise of your real estate agent, there may be a few things that you will modify or have multiple searches with different combination of keywords. The suggested requirements are what we have found to give us the best results. With this search in place, you will be notified when properties come up matching the keywords that you have specified. By studying the results of the search you will slowly gain a feeling as to what the market is like for that specific type of property. You also will recognize what a good deal is in the area versus what a great deal is in the area. At the same time, make sure that you have specified to your real estate agent that you are indeed very interested in moving on a property if the right property arises. Therefore, if anything comes across your real estate agent's desk you will be the first to know before the property gets listed.

Suggested Keywords for Search:

Vacant, Newly Renovated, Motivated Seller, Investor Alert, Cashflow property, Just Reduced, Bring Offers, Basement fully finished, In-Law Suite, Must Sell and Priced-to-Sell.

What Is Nearby?

As you are getting an idea as to what the market is in the area that you have targeted, you also would like to get to know the area itself.

> What is near the area?
> Where are the schools?
> What grades are the schools teaching?
> Where are the transit lines?
> Where are the grocery stores?
> What restaurants are nearby?

Imagine if you were to buy a property to live in, what would you look for and ask about? Put yourself in the shoes of your future renters and visualize what they will need to find out if they were living there and find out for yourself. The more you know about the area, the better you can show to a potential tenant why renting in that area is good. To do this, you can either search online or simply go to the area or community and drive around. Get a feel for what it is like to live there. Drive a few different routes to main roads and look for gas stations and fast food joints and mail boxes. This also is an opportunity for you to use your networking skills. Park your car and walk around the community. Talk to the neighbors and ask them what they like or not like about living there. Tell them that you are thinking of buying a property in the area and want to know more about it. Ask if there are any community gatherings or information sheets about the area. As you get familiarized with the community you will develop a sense as to why living in the area is good in which you can then tell your tenant.

Work with your TEAM

As big a role as your real estate agent will have at this time, another two members of your power team will be very important: your mortgage broker and lawyer. Like your real estate agent, you must work hand-in-hand with your mortgage broker and lawyer. They need to know what your plans are so that they can assist you the best way possible.

Mortgage Broker

If you have gotten a great mortgage broker, he or she will be able to tell you what the best rates are at that given time and what is happening with the laws of mortgages. They will be able to present you options as to what is the best product or best lender that you should go with for your property. For your future property transactions to run smoothly, one should have everything set up with their broker so that you know exactly what you can get. Discuss with your broker what your plans are and have them analyze your credit and qualifying power. Setting up this session with your broker will allow you to have a good idea as to what you should look for and what to expect when you find it. You will be required to provide the following (minimum):

- To fill out a form indicating all your assets and liabilities
- Couple of your current paystubs
- An employment letter as proof of your income

Do not leave out information. When you go to a doctor's office, you wouldn't leave out the fact that your throat hurts if the reason you are seeing him or her is because you want a cure for your throat would you? Likewise, if you do not disclose truthfully what your financial situation is, then the mortgage broker will not be able to help you to their fullest in giving you your best options. The last thing that you would like is for a deal to be all done and in the end, fall through due to you giving misleading information to your broker, which not only causes you to lose out on a deal but also challenges the trust between you and your broker. Having a great mortgage broker can do wonders for you and therefore, if you work closely with yours, you will have financing options that you never even thought you would have.

The following is a sample application that would be required by your mortgage broker (to download a copy of this sample of an application form courtesy of Raeann Lefebvre of Keystone Mortgages for easier viewing, go to www.makemoreworklessbook.com/cashflow):

Mortgage Application

Attention: **Raeann Lefebvre**
Tel: 780-914-2620
Fax   1-866-827-6172
Email: raeann@mortgageengineer.ca

Applicant One

Title	First Name		Mid Initial
Last Name			Suffix
Home Phone			
Work Phone			
Current Address			
Unit Number			
City			Province
Postal Code		Own / Rent	Years There
Birth Date	Month	Day	Year
SIN #			

Marital Status	Married / Common Law	Single / Engaged [X]	Separated/Divorced / Widowed

Number of Dependants (excluding Spouse)

Applicant Two

Title	First Name		Mid Initial
Last Name			Suffix
Home Phone			
Work Phone			
Current Address			
Unit Number			
City			Province
Postal Code		Own / Rent	Years There
Birth Date	Month	Day	Year
SIN #			

Relationship To Borrower	Spouse / Fiance	Co-Investor / Common Law	Co-Habit / Co-Signor

Other

If "Current Address" is less 3 years please provide a "Previous Address."

Previous Address		Unit Number		Previous Address		Unit Number
City		Province		City		Province
Postal Code	Own / Rent	Years There		Postal Code	Own / Rent	Years There

Notes

1. Birth date and Social Insurance Numbers are required for all applicants, if primary applicant is married, then disclosure of primary applicant's spouse is required

2. If income noted on top of page two is other than salary, please provide details. For example, if hourly wage, indicate the minimum number of hours worked for each week and the hourly rate, or if any income is from commission, please provide details of base salary, if any, and commissions earned per year for last two years.

PLEASE SIGN ON PAGE 3 AND RETURN APPLICATION WITH SIGNATURES TO RAEANN LEFEBVRE

Figure: 5-1 – Sample Mortgage Application Page 1
(courtesy of Keystone Mortgages)

MAKE MORE WORK LESS with CASHFLOW

PAGE 2

Requested Mortgage Details:
Mortgage Amount required: $
Purchase Price or Current Value: $
Down Payment Amount: $
Closing Date:
Day/ Month/ Year

	Applicant One	Applicant Two
Current Employer		
Address		
City, Province		
Job Title/Position		
Years There		

If "Current Employer" is less than 3 years please provide a "Previous Employer"

Previous Employer		
Address		
City, Province		
Job Title/Position		
Years There		

Annual Salary
Other Income
Total Income Primary Applicant and Co-Borrower

Assets		Liabilities	Bank Name	Payment/Month	Total Debt
Cash/Savings Account		Personal Loan			
Credit Union Deposits		Personal Loan			
Real Estate Deposits		Auto Lease			
Bonds (Market Value)		Mortgage(s) to remain			
Stocks (Market Value)		on OTHER properties			
Real Estate (Market Value)		Credit Cards			
Automobiles (Market Value)		Charge Account			
Personal Effects		Other			
RRSP		Other			
Other					
Other		Mortgage(s) to remain on SUBJECT property			
Automobiles Yr/Make & Model		Mortgage			
		Rent			
Total Assets		Other			
Current Net Worth		Other			
		Total Liabilities	Applied to TDSR		

Bank/Trust name
Branch Location
Account Number

Solicitor's Firm
Solicitor's Name
Street Address
City
Province, Postal Code
Phone Number
Fax Number

NOTE: Obtain a sample "VOID" cheque if client wants payment to come from "Bank" account.

Have you declared bankruptcy in the last 7 years?
Have you co-signed any other loans?

Figure: 5-2 – Sample Mortgage Application Page 2
(courtesy of Keystone Mortgages)

104

Client Application Authorization and Consent:

We, Mortgage Architects collect, receive, use and disclose personal information about you, our client, for the purposes of: verifying the information provided; assessing your credit-worthiness; maintaining our client relationship; presenting your mortgage application to various lenders and insurers for the purpose of securing and/or renewing a mortgage and/or related services and providing information to you about other products offered or approved by us, our affiliates, related entities or other third party financial partners that we believe may be of interest to you. We may also disclose your personal information under strict confidentiality restrictions to (i) any potential purchaser of our business and their advisors, (ii) any third party service providers to whom we may outsource our business functions and (iii) any parties involved in the securitization, assignment or pledge of loan(s)/ mortgage(s) that are obtained through us.

By signing this form, you consent to our collecting, using and disclosing your personal information for the foregoing purposes, and to carry out these purposes you agree that we may disclose your personal information to and receive your personal information from: consumer reporting agencies, credit bureaus, real estate appraisers, your bank(s) or other financial institutions with whom you have or have had dealings, your past mortage brokers, your present and past employers and such other third parties who may have information about your financial status. If there is more than one applicant, you also agree that we may collect, use and disclosure personal information about each of you from the other for the purposes listed above.

If you do not wish to receive any information on any other products offered or approved by us, and providing information to you about other products offered or approved by us, our affiliates, related entities or other third party financial partners that we believe may be of interest to you, please initial the box where indicated [or indicate your refusal verbally].

☐ **NO, you may not send me any information on other products**

You hereby agree that Mortgage Architects and your independent mortgage planner may use and retain your personal information for the forgoing purposes for seven (7) years after the later of a) the date of your latest application to us, and b) the date that all of your loans/mortgages contracted through us have expired or were terminated. Our privacy policies and procedures summary is on our website: **www.mortgagearchitects.ca**

APPLICANT: (Please tick one box only)   **CO-APPLICANT** (Please tick one box only)

Box 1 ☐ I wish to receive further information about life, disability and critical illness insurance coverage from Mortgage Architects   Box 1 ☐ I wish to receive further information about life, disability and critical illness insurance coverage from Mortgage Architects

OR

Box 2 ☐ I decline the opportunity to receive further information about life, disability and/or critical illness coverage from Mortgage Architects.   Box 2 ☐ I decline the opportunity to receive further information about life, disability and/or critical illness insurance from Mortgage Architects.

If Box 1 has been selected, please provide the following information:

Applicant | Day Mth Yr   **Co-Applicant** | Day Mth Yr

Date of Birth / Mortgage amount / Telephone

Smoker ☐ Non Smoker ☐   Smoker ☐ Non Smoker ☐

I/we understand that the terms and conditions of qualifying for coverage under such insurance are determined by the insurer, and that no such insurance will be in place unless and until I/we are so notified by the insurer.

25-Jan-11

Name of Applicant | Date   Co-Applicant Name | Date

Applicant Signature | Date   Co-Applicant Signature | Date

Office Use only: Yes ☐ No ☐

Expert File Name and Number | CRM Program   Broker Name/Signature | Date

Figure: 5-3 – Sample Mortgage Application Page 3
(courtesy of Keystone Mortgages)

Lawyer

Your lawyer is also a person that is very important at this time. They are the ones who can help you correctly set up your transactions on properties. If your company is set up correctly from the beginning, you will avoid many potential problems that could have come your way. Explain to your lawyer what your plans are, what your current goals are so that he or she can assess the best way for you to protect yourself. This also is the time when you should ask what conditions or clauses that you should have in your purchase contracts (these will be discussed later in this book). A big key to real estate investing is risk management. As long as you have the right exit strategies in place, you will reduce the amount of risk a certain opportunity can present. This way you will never get into a deal without being fully certain that it is the deal for you.

Once you have a good understanding with your lawyer, mortgage broker and your real estate agent, you are well prepared to analyze properties that will allow you to Make More and Work Less with Cashflow.

Knowing your exit strategies and having the team around you is like having a GPS leading you in the right direction to success.

Chapter 5 – Know Your Market Part I: Be Aware of What You Can Do

In much of society, research means to investigate something you do not know or understand.

- Neil Armstrong -

Assurance Keys to Your Success

- Four main exit strategies:
    o Wholesaling
    o Rent-to-Own
    o Buy-Fix-Flip
    o Buy-Hold

- Discuss with your real estate agent about what you want and set up searches

- Familiarize yourself with the area, drive by and ask yourself questions

- Discuss your plan with your mortgage broker and lawyer

Chapter - 6 -

Know Your Market Part II:
Acquire Properties Carefully

**If you are not willing to risk the unusual,
you will have to settle for the ordinary.**

- Jim Rohn -

*We've talked to our broker, lawyers and real estate
agent. We have been getting a lot of listings coming in
from the search that we set up. It's getting a little
overwhelming, how do you filter through all the listings
and properties?" asked Melissa shortly after their search
was set.*

Research

Now that you have everything in place, it is time to determine which properties fit your criteria. Everything that comes from the search is not worth putting an offer on. As we have discussed before, we will be focusing on cashflowing properties and therefore, will go through what we believe are signs of a good cashflow property.

After some time studying the results of the searches, you start to have a feel as to which properties are priced below market value and which properties have potential of being good opportunities. Properties that are listed below market price within their respective areas are a good sign of a motivated seller. Look for properties that have just been listed or have been listed for more than 90 days. Properties that just got listed will be fresh and therefore, you may be able to get there before other investors see them. One disadvantage with these properties is that because they have just been listed, the likeliness that the seller is willing to come down on their price is rare. They believe that their price is fair and will be firm at first. Whether the price is fair or not will be decided by you. Do not allow the seller or the seller's agent or your own agent to tell you otherwise. In the end, you are the buyer and the expert and therefore, you will determine what is a fair price for you, to buy the property. Keywords such as "motivated," "great potential," "cashflow opportunity", and "investor's opportunity" are all flags that should tweak your interest in the property. Looking at photos also is another great source in determining if the property is good for you.

- Do the pictures show that a lot of work is needed?
- Could it be good for another strategy?
- Do the pictures show that it is rent ready?
- Does the property look attractive to people from the outside?
- Are there two kitchens (One kitchen on the main floor, one kitchen in the basement)?
- Are the kitchens and bathrooms dated?

By looking at the pictures, one can get an idea as to why the property is listed for the price it is. With the combined triggers that we discussed here, you should now be able to select a few properties for further assessment.

With the properties that you have selected from the bunch that comes through searches, you can now determine which of these properties is worth seeing. If you are confident that the property doesn't require a viewing you may choose to put in an offer right away so that time isn't wasted. Remember, as long as the right clauses are in place, putting in an offer at this time is not uncommon. As for those that require a little more analysis, the following steps will allow you to determine if the property you have selected is worth seeing in person.

The following is a sample listing (for easier viewing, go to www.makemoreworklessbook.com/cashflow):

Residential							A		LP: $ 249,900

Status: A
Area: Edmonton
Community: Balwin 102000
Style: Bungalow
Zone: Zone 02
Year Built: 1957

MLS#:
Postal Code:
Linc #:
Type: Residential Detached Single Family
New Home on Old Lot: **Remod:**
Finish Lvls: 2

Mortgage: $ 0 **Cash Down:** **Due:** **Rate:**
Payments: **Lender:**
Legal Plan: **Blk/UF:** **Lot/Unit:**

Prop Class: Single Family
Look no more! This raised bungalow home offers 3 bedrooms, bright living room, and eat in kitchen. This Fully Finished in-law Basement Suite comes with TWO SEPARATE ENTRANCE'S. HUGE Windows, Large Bedroom, a kitchen, 3 piece bathroom, and a large living room. Seperate Laundry Room. This House is on a Large Lot and has a Double Detached Garage. Upgrades include: windows, exterior stucco, furnace, hot water tank, 100 AMP electrical, eavestrough, plumbing and upgraded attic insulation, laminate flooring upstairs and downstairs. Just minutes to the Yellow Head Trail, Anthony Henday, and 82 Street, 66 Street. Close to all amenities. Great revenue property or mortgage helper.

Virtual Tour: **Brochure:**

	1Pc	2Pc	3Pc	4Pc	5Pc	6Pc			**Directions:**		
Baths:	0	0	1	1	0	0	**Elem School:**				
Ensuite Bth:	0	0	0	0	0	0	**Jr/Mid Schl:**				
Bdrms Abv:	2 Total Bdrms: 3		**Addl Rms:**				**High Schl:**				
Fin FP/Rgh-In:		**Fpl Fuel:**					**Other Schl:**		**Schl Bus:**	N	
Parking:	Double Garage Detached						**Garage:**	Yes	**Level**	Mtr2	SqFt
									Main Lvl:		
Living Room:			**Master Bedrm:**	M					**Upper:**		
Dining Room:			**Bedrm 2:**	M					**Above Grd:**		
Kitchen:			**Bedrm 3:**	B					**Lower Lvl:**		
Family Room:			**Bedrm 4:**						**Below Grd:**		
Den:									**Total A.G.:**	80.0	861.12

Flooring:	Laminate Flooring	**Roof Type:**	Asphalt Shingles
Foundation:	Concrete	**Fireplace:**	
Exterior:	Stucco	**Construction:**	Wood Frame
Heating Type:	Forced Air-1	**Basement:**	Full
Features:		**Bsmt Dev:**	Suite
		Heat Fuel:	Natural Gas
Goods Incl:	DRYER, REFRG, REFR2, STVS2, STVEL, WASHR	**Goods Excluded:**	

Site Infl:	LANE, PLAY, POOLP, PRIV, SHOP, SCHLS, TRANS	**Lot Shape:**	Rectangular	**Front Exp:** West
		Frntg X Dpth:		
Amenities:		**Zoning/Land Use:**		
		Conform:		
		Tax Amt/Yr :	$ 1,600 / 2011	**LI:**
Restrictions:	N-KNW	**Warranty :**		

Condo Name:		**Ownership:** PRIV	**Condo:**	**HOA:**
Prk Encl/Unit/Type: 2		**Incl:**		
Prk Plan Desc:		**Registered Size:**		

Seller:		**Appt:** APPT		
List Realtor:		**Appointment Ph:**	**List Date:**	06/22/12
List Realtor Email:		**List Realtor Web:**		
List Firm:			**Occupancy:**	
List Realtor2:			**Possession:** /15day/nego	**Exclusion:** N
List Firm2:		**Comm:**		**SRR:** N

Pend Date:	**Sold Date:**	**Sold Price:**	**DOM:** 3 days	**Entered:** 06/22/12
Sold Term:			**Disc:**	**Expiry Date:**
Sell Firm:				**Sell Firm 2:**
Sell Agent:				**Sell Agent 2:**

06/25/12	8:52 AM	INFORMATION HEREIN DEEMED RELIABLE BUT NOT GUARANTEED	RES Agent Detail View

Figure: 6-1 – Sample Listing (courtesy of MLS.ca)

Get Comparables

One of the first things that you must do after you have a target property is to have your real estate agent do a comparable on that property. A comparable is where your real estate agent will do a search of all the properties within the same area, with the same sort of property with regards to size and number of bedrooms and bathrooms that were sold within the last three to six months. Since real estate runs in a cycle throughout the year, the fair market value actually changes all the time. In general, we have a seller's market during the spring and fall seasons and a buyer's market during the summer and winter seasons. This is usually due to the tendencies that people do not like moving during the cold days of winter and during vacation times of summer and contrastingly would usually like to settle into their new homes before the school year starts during the fall season and once snow melts during the spring season. Again, once you are able to place yourself in the shoes of those you would like to help, you will be able to place yourself further ahead than those who don't. Since the market changes all the time, an accurate comparable is very important. The comparable will tell you what the property you are targeting is worth, with respect to those around it, assuming that it is in proper condition.

If you would like to make a further assessment of the value, select five of the closest matching properties from the comparables, in distance and in size, take the sum of all five and divide it by the total size of all five and then multiply this number by the size of your target property.

For Example:

Your target property size = 1100 square feet, three bedrooms

	Distance	Size	Sale Price	# of bedrooms
Comparable 1	5 blocks	900	$250,000	2
Comparable 2	10 blocks	1300	$375,000	4
Comparable 3	2 blocks	1050	$280,000	3
Comparable 4	8 blocks	1200	$330,000	3
Comparable 5	20 blocks	1000	$300,000	3
Comparable 6	14 blocks	975	$260,000	2
Comparable 7	33 blocks	800	$255,000	2

Based on the comparables, the best comparable is No. 3 meaning your target property is worth about $280,000.

Based on the other comparables we also can say that Comparables: 1, 3, 4, 5 and 6 are closely matched to our target property. Therefore, if we take the total sum of the sale prices

Total of top five properties $250,000
    + $280,000
    + $330,000
    + $300,000
    + $260,000
    $1,420,000

Now divide it by the sum of the sizes
= 900+1050+1200+1000+975 = 5125 square feet

We get $277.07 per square foot.

Therefore, we can say that our target property is worth about 1,100 square feet times $277.07 = $304,777

Here is a sample comparable (for easier viewing, go to www.makemoreworklessbook.com/cashflow):

Comparable Address	# Beds	SqFt	Days on Market	List Price	Sale Price
2032 47 ST	4	1165.74	45	$269,900	$269,000
2112 54 ST	3	995.67	20	$289,000	$272,000
6308 17 AV	4	1173.28		$303,900	
1788 48 ST NW	5	1040.88	47	$305,000	$286,000
2032 47 ST	5	1165.74		$319,900	
2103 54 ST NW	5	1180.81		$325,000	
2111 35 ST	5	1091.47	25	$329,000	$318,000
1023 55 ST	5	1243.24	10	$329,900	$326,500
444 KNOTTWOOD RD W	5	1229.25		$329,900	
1511 75 ST	5	1182.10	27	$329,900	$322,000
6237 13 AV	6	1018.60	51	$329,900	$320,000
1979 68 ST	3	1629.67	43	$339,000	$325,000
4604 10 AV	5	1097.93	60	$339,000	$325,000
1935 61 ST	6	1173.28	101	$339,900	$338,900
3527 13 AV NW	4	1128.07		$344,500	
3920 19 AV	5	1196.96	65	$344,900	$330,000
2020 82 ST	6	1413.64	11	$359,800	$354,000
1820 65 ST NW	5	1474.67	13	$368,800	$358,500
5522 11A AV	6	2098.98		$379,900	
1925 89 ST	3	2097.80	87	$379,900	$367,000

Figure: 6-2 – Sample Comparable (courtesy of Josh Tesolin - Realtor)

There is no right answer here, but both numbers are very important. As a buyer, you would look at the more conservative number of $280,000 and therefore, when questioned about why you think it is worth that much you will be able to show them why. As a seller, you would set your price at $304,000. In our situation, we would like to make sure that the property of interest will be profitable. Therefore, the more conservative $280,000 will be used.

Now that you have a comparative value for the property you are targeting, it is always good to take a look at what the city assessed the property at as well. Note that the city assessment is usually a year behind, so depending on what the value is you may use it to your advantage or not. For example, if the city assessment shows that the property is worth $275,000 you may want to use that to show the seller that their listed value of $290,000 is too high. Vice versa, if the city assessed it at $300,000, you may not want to use the value during the buying stage but at the selling stage of the opportunity. For the purpose of our example, let's use the city assessed value of $275,000. In comparison to our comparable of $280,000, assuming that our target property is worth the more conservative value of $275,000 would be best.

Here is a sample of what a city assessment looks like (for easier viewing, go to www.makemoreworklessbook.com/cashflow):

000	225500			238000	265
	334000		222500		246
500	129500		231500	210000	
500	168000		232500	208500	251
	200000		256500	199000	225
000	246000		140500	245500	265
000	189500		164500	226000	
000	239500		230000	174500	175
500	121000		101000	104500	
000	121000		121000	122000	
500	128000		129000	130500	
	70000				
	70000				

Tax Roll:
Assessed Value: $230,000
100% Taxable: Yes
100% Complete: Yes
Neighbourhood: Balwin
Property Type: Residential
Land Use: 100% Single Family Dwelling
Lot Size: 525.019 M2 / 5651.4 FT2 / .13 AC
Building Count: 1
Year Built, Building Class: 1957, Bungalow With Basement
Approx Living Area: 72.25 M2 / 777.7 FT2
(Does not include basement area or 3rd level of split level)
Basement Development: Yes
Garage: Yes
Fireplace: No
Walkout Basement: No
Air Conditioning: No

Figure: 6-3 – Sample City Assessment (courtesy of City of Edmonton)

118

Estimating your Expenses

Knowing the worth of the property, you can now determine what the monthly expenses will be for the property. Assuming that you purchase the property at $275,000, you can now determine the mortgage payments. After consulting with your mortgage broker, you will know what the going rates are and length of amortization period. As we are not mortgage brokers, we can only do a quick calculation as to what the mortgage payments would be. Let's say you put a 20 percent down payment on the property, which, in most cases, is required for an investment property, with a 25 year amortization at a rate of 3.5 percent, you can expect a mortgage payment of about $1,100. This is both interest and principle payment combined. To get the average rates and amortization term, one can always check online or call your broker. To calculate the mortgage payments, there are free apps that you can download on your phone and online sites that can calculate mortgage payments for you (www.mortgagecalculator.org/). Note, that there are many different mortgage products out there, and therefore, consulting with your broker is best. However, at this stage, the information that you have will be sufficient.

To determine the monthly expenses for a house there are four important keys to remember: **P.I.T.I.**

> **P**rinciple
> **I**nterest
> **T**ax
> **I**nsurance

We have just discussed how the principle and interest is determined, now for the tax and insurance portions. The tax that we are referring to is the property tax that the government charges. This value is usually available in the listing. If not, you can always find matching properties and use that value for this process. People like discussing how unhappy they are about taxes, so if you would like, you can ask around the area about what they are paying in taxes as well. Generally, we find that using an assumed number or the listed value is sufficient

Finally insurance, you can call your insurance company to get a better idea of how much a house of that nature would cost for rental insurance.

Something that many investors do not account for is the miscellaneous expenses and the vacancies that one will encounter. You never know when something comes up and something needs to be fixed or if your tenant moves out and you need to find a new tenant. We generally account for 5 percent of the rent for miscellaneous expenses and another 5 percent of the rent for vacancy. Accounting for these into your monthly expenses now, will allow you to be prepared for things down the road if they ever happen. The reason a lot of investors lose money as landlords is that they do not account for these expenses and therefore, charge too little rent or have bought a property that doesn't cashflow. If the property taxes or condo fees rise, whatever cashflow they thought they had would be gone. Having these expenses factored in will allow you to have a cushion to fall back on if need be, if not then you will have more cashflow than you anticipated!

What is the Going Rent?

So how do we determine the rent market? Search online or ask your team member, the property manager. There are numerous sites online set up for people looking to rent. Just think if you were a renter where would you go to look for a property like the one you have? Go searching for basement suites and main floor rentals that match the criteria of your target property. Community, size, number of bedrooms, number of bathrooms, garage are some of the main searches that you will use. Your property manager also should be able to give you some ball park range as to how much to rent your target property. After a while you will get a pretty good idea as to what the rent market is like. Unlike the prices for properties, the rent market doesn't vary as much within a city. The garage and pet fees are discussed later.

My Cashflow

At this time, you should have all the information you need to determine whether or not the property you are targeting will cashflow and if it is worth seeing in person. With the example that we have been using, let's see if the property is worth considering.

Property Value: List Price = $290,000
                                         Comparables = $275,000

Income: Main Floor rent = $1,300
                                          Basement rent = $900

Expenses: Principle & Interest = $1100
                                                    Taxes = $200
                                                 Insurance = $60
                                     5 percent vacancy = $110
                           5 percent miscellaneous = $110
                              Total Monthly Income = $2,200
                         Total Monthly Expenses = $1,580

Total Monthly Cashflow = $620

If you were to pick up this property for $275,000 at 20 percent, you would have spent $55,000 and that means you'll get a return on investment of $620X12 / $55,000 = 13.5 percent a year!

Based on our experience, any property with the potential of having a cashflow of more than $500 a month is worth viewing. In most cases, anything that cashflows more than $200 is desirable; however, if we would like to have partners or do joint ventures on deals and also to protect ourselves from increases to taxes or fees, anything less than $500/month will be too small to split among the parties and is too risky.

What If?

Always have a backup plan in place. If, for whatever reason, you are not able to find renters for the property, you can always put the property back on the market and sell at a profit. Therefore, you should calculate another set of numbers. At what price would you need to purchase the property so that you can turn around and sell the property in three to six months without losing money and possibly even make money? Since you have all the information on the monthly expenses you can now determine how much your carrying cost would be if you were to sell the property while not having tenants.

Let's assume that we need to sell the above-mentioned property. You are confident that you can sell it for $280,000 within four months. Therefore, for you to come out even, you will need to purchase the property for:

Sale price = $280,000

Holding cost = $1,360 X four months
(Principle + Interest + Property Tax + Insurance)

Lawyer fees = $2000

Real estate agent fees = $12,400
(7 percent for the first $100,000 and 3 percent for the remainder, may be different depending on where you are)

Your Purchase price = $260,160 to break even.

In most cases, it will not be worth your time if you are going to be selling the property; however, this value may allow you to determine where you want to start or end with your offers. You also can negotiate the fees of your real estate agent and lawyer. We do not recommend this until you have built a relationship with them first.

By doing the research and analysis consistently, you will find that picking out good deals will come easier and easier. With more practice, you will be able to look at properties and know if a deal is there or not within minutes. Set up spreadsheets and checklists for yourself so that the process is smoother and simpler or use one of ours. As another added bonus to you, we have included a sample template of our very own cashflow analysis. Use it or modify it to your liking so that you can find the right properties that will enable you to Make More and Work Less with Cashflow. Go to www.makemoreworklessbook.com/cashflow to download your template.

Here is a sample template:

PROPERTY INFORMATION			
House Style	Bungalow	Main (# Bed / # Bath)	3 / 2
Address	1234 12 Ave	Basement (# Bed / # Bath)	2 / 1
Neighbourhood	Minchau	Main Square Footage	1200
Asking Price	$340,000.00	Basement Square Footage	1000
www.yourarea.ca		www.makemoreworklessbook.com	

	Lease Option	Buy, Fix, Flip	Buy, Fix, Hold
PURCHASING			
Purchase Price	$350,000.00	$180,000.00	$350,000.00
Down Payment (DP) Percentage	20%	20%	20%
Legal	$2,000.00	$2,000.00	$2,000.00
Inspections	$600.00	$600.00	$600.00
Appraisal	$300.00	$300.00	$300.00
Total Cash to Close	**$72,900.00**	**$38,900.00**	**$72,900.00**
INCOME			
Monthly Main Level Rent	$1,350.00		$1,350.00
Monthly Basement Level Rent	$1,150.00		$1,150.00
Monthly Garage Rent	$200.00		$200.00
Monthly Pet Fee	$50.00		$50.00
Monthly Rent Credit (for Lease Option)	$302.02		
Total Monthly Income	**$3,052.02**		**$2,750.00**
EXPENSES			
Cleaning	$300.00	$300.00	$300.00
Renovation Cost	$5,000.00	$60,000.00	$5,000.00
Holding Period		4	
Realtor Fee	$15,473.63	$14,500.00	
Monthly Expenses			
Mortgage Payment	$1,336.76	$687.48	$1,336.76
Principle	$280,000.00	$144,000.00	$280,000.00
Interest Rate	4.00%	4.00%	4.00%
Ammortization in years	30	30	30
Property Tax	$250.00	$250.00	$250.00
Utilities (Tenants usually pay)		$450.00	
Home Insurance	$75.00	$75.00	$75.00
Condo Fee (If applicable)	$0.00	$0.00	$0.00
Misc. (Vacancy/repairs. 10% of gross rent)	$305.20		$275.00
Contingency Fund (10% of gross rent)	$305.20		$275.00
Total Monthly Expense	**$2,272.17**	**$1,462.48**	**$2,211.76**
Total Expense		**$80,649.91**	
Net Monthly Cashflow	**$779.85**		**$538.24**
SELLING / LEASE TERMS			
Estimated Selling Price	$382,454.45	$350,000.00	
Lease period in years (~3-5 years)	3		
Option consideration (~3 months rent)	$8,250.00		
Tenant Buyer's Required DP	5%		
Remaining Mortgage after lease period	$264,596.43		
SUMMARY			
Total Cash Required	**$78,200.00**	**$119,549.91**	**$78,200.00**
Net Profit	**$75,011.67**	**$86,450.09**	
Annual Cashflow	**$9,358.24**		**$6,458.85**
ROI	**95.92%**	**72.31%**	**8.26%**
NOTES			
1) For wholesale, use the "Buy, Fix, Flip" column and charge according to the profit the investor will make			
2) Fill out the "Buy, Fix, Hold" and "Buy, Fix, Flip" columns to populate all other columns			
3) Profit is dependent on user			

Figure: 6-4 – Sample Template (courtesy of AREA)

Competition

Please note that listed properties have a lot of competition. Sellers using this method also may be less motivated and may be less willing to negotiate on price. Good-to-great opportunities will usually come to you in a form of a referral or a lead. Whether this is from people that you have been networking with or someone calling on an ad that you have posted or someone sending you information through your Web site, opportunities can come to you in all shapes and sizes. With your knowledge about certain areas that you have targeted, you are now equipped to determine if these leads are good or great deals.

With the right amount of knowledge you will be confident in your numbers and feelings, when putting an offer on a property that will help you Make More and Work Less with Cashflow.

Research is a form of risk management.

Manage your risk before making your final decisions.

Chapter 6 - Know Your Market Part II: Acquire Properties Carefully

As a research tool, the internet is invaluable.

- Noam Chomsky -

Assurance Keys to Your Success

- Get comparables for your property and determine what the property is worth

- Determine your expenses: PITI + Miscell.

  o Principle
  o Interest
  o Taxes
  o Insurance
  o 5% Vacancy
  o 5% Miscellaneous

- Determine market rent

- Determine your cashflow

- Manage your risk

- Have multiple streams of property leads

MAKE MORE WORK LESS with CASHFLOW

128

Chapter - 7 -

Property Viewings:
Let's See What We Have

**It had long since come to my attention
that people of accomplishment rarely
sat back and let things happen to them.
They went out and happened to things**

- Leonardo Da Vinci -

*It wasn't long after our conversation with John about
setting up searches and how to assess the numbers
when John called us excitedly and said, "We found a few
places! The numbers look good and the cashflow
potential is great! Now, what do we do?" We told him
that the next step is to go look at the properties.*

Now that we have a targeted property, the next step is to see if the property is everything we expect it to be. Never judge a book by its cover, but remember that the cover is what got your initial interest. Pictures and descriptions can be deceiving. You never know what people are hiding. It is at this time when we are able to determine what a starting offer can be. Depending on the condition of the property you may want to re-evaluate your purchase price or exit strategy. To save yourself and your real estate agent's time, it is always beneficial for everyone to have multiple properties lined up for viewing. That way, not only can you hit multiple viewings in one outing but also have a chance to compare the properties as they are all fresh in everyone's head. During this time you will also have the opportunity to build your relationship with your real estate agent. Get their opinion on the properties and ask what they usually seek. In general, a good-and-experienced real estate agent will have no issues sharing their tips with you as long as you are there to add value to them in the future.

Setting up Viewings

After you have gotten three to six properties chosen, contact your real estate agent and see what they think about the properties. Have them set up viewing appointments and while doing so, get a feel of the property. Since the person is usually another agent, the selling agent, a good real estate agent will be able to "read between the lines" of the selling agent's responses. Questions such as: Why are the owners selling? Why hasn't the property sold yet? And how much activity have you gotten on the property? Are good "feeler" questions to ask. You can always take it upon yourself to call the properties; however, if you do so, you will usually be stuck in a situation where the seller agent also will become your buying agent which causes a sticky situation. Having your real estate agent act on your behalf also is advantageous as he or she will be there to negotiate for you. A good-to-great real estate agent will understand the investor's mind and therefore, will stand by your numbers. By having your real estate agent be part of your buying process also is adding value to them. This is because they will then get a share of the seller's commission for getting the property sold if you indeed end up purchasing the property. Other useful questions to have asked are: Is the property rented? How much is rent? Do the tenants prefer to stay? Is there a separate entrance to the basement? Is there a potential for a complete basement suite? The more you know about the property, the better equipped you are when you go to view the property. It also will give you a chance to gauge whether the seller is open to sharing information or not or for you to verify the information when you go to the property.

There are four main categories of items that you will want to look for while you are at the property: Exterior, Interior, basement interior and hidden interior.

Exterior: What to Look For

The first thing we would do when we see a property is take in the surroundings. What did you see as you were driving to the property? What did the houses near it look like? How close is the property to a busy road? How does the property look in comparison to the properties on the same street? All these questions will determine the rent-ability and the re-salability of the property, when and if, the time comes. Take a walk around the property and take note of the following items:

- Where are the trees?
- Are they close to the property?
- Are the trees taking away from the look of the house?
- How is the condition of the roof?
- Is the ground sloped correctly for drainage?
- What is the condition of the concrete, driveway or walkway?
- Is drainage sloped away from the house?
- What is the condition of the walls and foundations?
- Are there cracks?
- What is the condition of the garage or the fence?
- Is there a garage or a shed?
- If no garage - is there room for a garage?
- How are the gutters?
- What's the condition of the lawn?
- Are the window wells in the right locations?
- Are there anything obstructing the basement windows?
- How big are the basement windows?

What you see may re-determine what you are willing to offer. Most of the items here are not major issues except for the roof condition and drainage. If the roof needs repairing within one to two years, you may need to expect a major expense coming your way. If the sloping of grade is leading water toward the property, you can expect future water damage if there isn't any already, which will mean another large expense to repair and re-grade the property.

Remember to take notes and pictures of what you see, so that if need be, you can always call up contractors and trades to give you quotes and assessments as to how much it will cost you to fix certain items. If you choose to call for quotes, make sure you call a few to get a more accurate number that you may want to use for future negotiating. Now that you have completed your walk around the exterior you are on your way inside the house.

Interior: What to Look For

While indoors, make sure you take note of how you feel when you walk through the doors. Sometimes, a person's "gut" feel says a lot. If something doesn't feel right, it probably isn't. Take careful notes as to how the property is laid out.

- Is it practical?
- Would removing walls open the place up?
- What are the conditions of the bathrooms and kitchen?

Remember for a cashflow property, you would like to do as few renovations as possible. So while you are looking at the kitchen, bedrooms and bathrooms, ask yourself:

"Is this in livable condition right now?"

If minor changes are needed, take note of them.

- Do the carpets need cleaning or need to be replaced?
- Do the cabinets need replacing, refinishing or just a deep cleaning?
- Are the bathrooms clean?
- How does the house smell? Smoky?
- Are the appliances in working condition?
- Are there cracks in the walls?
- Is the carpet on top of hardwood flooring?
- What is the condition of the hardwood or laminate or tiles?

To see if there is original hardwood flooring, go look at a floor vent. Remove the cover and look at the floor layers.

- How are the hardware conditions?
- Light switches and door handles and cabinet knobs, do they need replacing?
- What are the conditions of the windows? Are there leaks? Frost? Cracks?

The following will be very important when it comes to cashflow properties, and it is usually what makes or breaks the deal.

Is there a logical separate entrance for the basement? If not existing, will it be easy to do? Whether by adding a wall or door?

A separate entrance basically means that: a tenant in the basement can access their unit without going through the main floor unit and vice versa. If the basement entrance is in the middle of the main floor, chances are great the property is not going to be a great cashflow property. However, there are instances where it can be done. A good saying to remember is: everything cashflows, depending on how you structure the deal.

The reason a basement floor unit is so important for a cashflow unit is because it reduces your risk and maximizes your profits and cashflow. You can generally get $200-$500 more by renting out a main floor and basement floor unit than the whole house on its own. Based on our example above, we are able to get $1,300 for the main and $900 for the basement floors for a total of $2,200 a month. The same house rented out as a whole may only get you $1,700-$1,800 a month. Not only does this get you more cashflow, but it also protects your bottom line by having two tenants. That way if one moves out, you will at least have a portion of your monthly expenses paid for by the other tenant, hence less money out of your pocket.

Interior: What to Look for In the Basement

We are now on our way to the basement.

- How is the layout for a potential separate entrance?
- How is the common area?
- Is there a logical space for laundry access for both the main and basement tenant?
- Can the main floor tenant access the laundry without going through the basement unit's space?
- If not, go back upstairs to see if you can place a laundry unit in a logical place

Be aware of where the existing main water lines are and if the washer and dryers can be stacked. If a lot of work is needed to run water to a new washer and dryer location on the main floor, the property may not be a good investment. The fact that washer and dryers can be stacked allows for an existing closet to be a potential location for the main floor laundry and saves space.

While in the basement take a look at the existing kitchen and bathroom if there is one. If not, make sure there is rough-ins for a potential kitchen or bathroom. This is yet another potential deal breaker. If the provisions for a kitchen or bathroom are not in-place you may need to consider looking at the next property unless of course you are able to pick up the property at a low enough price, so that developing the basement is accounted for.

- Is the basement developed enough for someone to live in as-is?
- Are the windows big enough for a person to get out of?

To have a basement suite to rent, the bedroom must have a window that is large enough for a person to leave, this is required by law as a safety measure in case of fire.

- Is the basement laid out so that living there is functional?
- How much work will be required to make the basement livable?

Now you will need to look at the hardware of the property.

- What are the conditions of the furnace and the hot water tank?
- What are the ages of them and when were they last checked?

A new hot water tank or furnace can put you back a few thousand dollars if you are not careful with your walkthrough. If all these questions are accounted for, you may have a great property within your grasp.

Hidden in the Walls: What to Look For

Before you get all excited about the prospect of landing on a goldmine, there are yet a few other items that you'll need to see that are hidden from plain view. You need to look at the electrical work.

- What is the wiring in the property? Is it up to code?
- Is it 60 amp or 100 amp service?
- Are the outlets grounded?
- How updated is the electrical panel?

These answers can be found by looking at the outlets and the electrical panel. If you are not careful, you might end up needing to replace all the electrical. For the purposes of a cashflow property, this may be a deal breaker; however, for a buy-fix-and-flip scenario, upgrading the electrical may increase the value of the property by a nice sum and also increase the re-salability of the property. Other items to notice are: cracks in the foundations of the basement, water stains, indentations in the floor, leaks to pipes and cracks in walls and ceiling.

There are a few different types of cracks to notice:

- Everyday wear-and-tear cracks
- Foundation horizontal cracks
- Foundation vertical cracks

Of the three, the one of most concern are the horizontal cracks. If you see these in the basement walls, chances are great there are foundation issues that will mean a deal breaker. All the other forms of cracks can be repaired and depending on how extreme the cracks are will determine how much you would like to spend on repairing them.

Water and plumbing issues are major elements that need to be addressed.

- Do you see rust or build up at the piping joints and connections?
- Do you see stains on the walls, ceiling or floors?

If so, the probability of a water problem exists or existed. Make sure that this was addressed. If you see stains on the basement walls then there may be a foundation issue where water is seeping in though the ground and walls.

- Are the water pipes up to code?
- Are they copper or lead piping?

Take note whether there is a separate metering system. This would allow you to monitor the water usage of the main and basement floors separately. In most cases, you will not see these installed; however, if you do, this is a huge bonus. For simplicity of managing tenants, you may choose to have something like that installed, but it is not a priority to do so.

Two very important items that may be within the walls of the property are mold and asbestos. If air born, these two items may cause serious health issues. Now before you take your hazmat suits from your closets, properties in general will not be hazardous places unless specified. Keep an eye for black coloring on floors, ceilings, walls and cabinets, usually in locations close to water, such as: bathrooms, kitchens and exterior water taps. As for asbestos, this issue is usually concealed within the walls, floors or in the attic. Depending on the age of the home, where asbestos was used for a lot of building materials, you may see asbestos potential materials all over the home. Do not be alarmed, as long as you do not go around disturbing the walls and punching holes, asbestos is not an issue. These issues will be noticed by a good inspection which will be discussed later in this book. The reason we are mentioning these items is so that you are aware of the potential of these hazards.

With experience and more practice, you will be able to identify a lot of potential issues and red flags throughout a property. Whether it is a potential problem affecting your cashflow, a problem affecting your cash investment or a potential health issue, you'll be able to identify them and address them as needed. At the beginning, this may be a very overwhelming task and sometimes scary, however as the saying goes, "action cures fears". To reduce uncertainty and risk, feel free to ask your real estate agent as you go through the property. An experienced real estate agent will be able to give you a lot of insight as to what you need to remember. If you choose to do it, you could arrange your team member – the contractor to come to the viewings with you for his or her opinion and advice. However, to respect everyone's time, bringing in your contractor may not be beneficial. Remember, at this stage, you are just getting a feel for what you should be offering for the property, not buying it. Generally, for a cashflow property, you should not spend more than $5,000 in renovations to get the property rent ready. If it comes to developing a basement, or more is needed, then make sure that you account for that in your offer (discussed in a later chapter) or in your cash investment and analysis of the deal. There are a lot of opportunities left to make sure the property is logical and safe to purchase.

More than Meets the Eye

To illustrate why one needs to take a look at a property before putting in an offer, we would like to share a few stories of properties that we have visited that was *"more than meets the eye."*

Based on pictures, we were very excited about a property, and prior to going to the site, we couldn't wait to put an offer on it to lock out the competition. According to the listing and the photos, we were pretty sure that there would be a separate entrance and a potential for a basement suite. On top of that, there was a hot tub installed and the basement was recently done. Having great expectations, we headed to the property and were greatly disappointed. Turns out, that one of the doors was a "fake" door. It literally opened to a wall! The work that was done in the basement had very poor workmanship and would have needed to be redone. Finally, the hot-tub was installed in the middle of a living room area! After looking at this property, we realized that it would need a lot more capital investment to put into the property than once thought and decided that it was not even worth an offer.

Another property that we have seen showed a lot of promise as well. The pictures showed clean and newly renovated interiors. Going to the property with high expectations, we were again looking at a disappointment. Turns out, the pictures were taken of only the certain areas that were fixed up and cleaned, whereas the rest of the property was an utter mess. The electrical work was outdated, and the layout just didn't fit for a cashflow property. Therefore, we didn't put an offer on this property.

Note that you will most likely be looking at a lot of properties that for whatever reason you do not end up buying. With time and persistence, you will see one that will be worth pursuing further. For instance, one of our most profitable properties had great potential based on pictures and its listing. Going to the viewing, we instantly knew that we had something of value. The interior was nicely redone and was modernized. A separate entrance was already there. A huge garage and a well-kept lawn were there as well. In the end, we only had to redo the common area where the laundry was. By adding a door for the basement unit, access to the laundry was made and we switched the side by side laundry units with a stackable pair. With just some minor changes and cleanup, we got a great cashflowing property and a set of laundry units to put in our other properties.

By having a good look at the properties that you have targeted, you will be able to envision whether or not the property has great potential to cashflow. When you have a good idea as to what work needs to be done and what to budget, you will mitigate your risks by accounting for the work in your offers or passing it up altogether. Do not let your emotions dictate your actions and let the numbers be your guide. There always will be opportunities. It is up to you to be persistent enough to find them. Finding the right properties will get you closer to your goal to Make More and Work Less with Cashflow.

Always verify what you read and see in pictures and descriptions. Going to the property will allow you to verify the seller's thoughts.

Chapter 7 – Property Viewings: Let's See What We Have

As I grow older, I pay less attention to what people say. I just watch what they do.

- Andrew Carnegie -

Assurance Keys to Your Success

- Pictures and descriptions can be deceiving – ask questions

- Have multiple properties lined up for viewing

- Do not have your buying agent be the selling agent

- Major Exterior Items: Roof and Grading

- Condition of Kitchen, Bathroom, Furnace and Hot Water Tank

- Basement suite, Separate Entrance and Laundry Access

- Hidden Items: Electrical, Water Lines and Horizontal Cracks

- Do not disturb walls and floors – potential mold and asbestos sites

- Assess your costs to determine your offer

Chapter - 8 -

Have No Fears:
Make Great Offers

Action cures fear.

- David J. Schwartz -

After a couple of days, John came over with a stack of papers and notes. He had multiple listing sheets, notes, comparables and a lost look on his face. "I looked at a handful of properties and have a pretty good idea of what the properties are worth. There are a couple of houses here that we'll like to purchase. Putting an offer on them is really scaring us. What are we suppose to do? How should we approach this?"

The Rule of 80-20

As we have addressed before, "Action cures fear." The fact that you have gotten this far, means that you already have conquered many of your fears. So don't stop now! Now is where all your preparation will go to the next stage. Remember, you will target more properties than you actually buy. A great concept to remember is *The Pareto Principle* (also known as the *80–20 rule*). This principle states that, for many events, roughly 80 percent of the effects come from 20 percent of the causes. For example, if you look at an insurance brokerage, 80 percent of their sales probably come from 20 percent of their agents. In associations, 80 percent of the work is done by 20 percent of the members. When applied to properties, for every 100 properties you see, maybe 20 are worth offering. Of that 20, 20 percent will be accepted. Of that 20 percent, 20 percent will be a good deal. When you look at your numbers, you will see that it is that elite 20 percent of deals that create 80 percent of your profits.

And/Or Assignee – Contingency No. 1

Before you do anything regarding filling out the contract offer, get your real estate agent to put your company name or personal name in the buyer section with the following "and/or assignee." By adding "and/or assignee," it gives you the opportunity to sell the contract. Some lenders do not prefer to have this added in the buyer's line, therefore have your real estate agent include it in the clauses of the contract. Even though you have no intentions of selling the contract, having this in your contract gives you the flexibility to do so if something arises. This is usually where a wholesale situation takes place where you have someone else sign the contact upon closing with the conditions that you have agreed to with the seller. An agreement between you and the assignee is that they get your contract for a fee. Requesting to have "and/or assignee" on your contract is one of many items that can be negotiated. You will find that it will never hurt to ask. The worst that can happen is having it rejected, and you end up with nothing, which is what you had if you didn't ask. So, no worse for wear.

What You Should Offer

We have done our numbers and viewed the property, next step is the offer. Based on the numbers, we know what the property is probably worth, how much we need for buying the property if we were to sell it within the next four months without a loss and also how much we are able to qualify for a loan or put as a down payment. You also have determined roughly how much you think you would need to put into the property for it to be a justifiable investment. Based on the research that you have done, you should be able to determine whether the asking price is fair or not. Using the previous example, this is what we know:

Asking price = $290,000
Fair Market Price = $275,000
Price at which you will come out even if you had to sell = $260,160

Assuming that there is less than $5,000 worth of renovations needed for the property to be rented, and for the purposes of a cashflow property, we know that it will cashflow at about $620 a month, a target price for this property would be between $270,000 and $280,000. Knowing this and knowing there will be some back and forth negotiating, a good initial offer of $260,000 would be a good place to start. Generally, we would like to offer a number that is two times the difference between their asking price and our target price. Therefore, in our scenario:

$290,000-$275,000 = $15,000
2 times $15,000 = $30,000
$290,000-$30,000 = $260,000 = starting offer

This is where you must take emotion from the property and the deal. Regardless of what people tell you, what the selling agent thinks and what the seller replies, you have your reasons for your numbers and at the end of the day, the investment is yours and you want your investment to be profitable. Also, you never know what the seller's motivation is. How motivated is the seller? What is the seller's bottom line? You will soon get a feel for this based on the response to your offer.

If the above said property was listed for say $260,000 and after the viewing, you figured that the property requires about $30,000 worth of renovations, then your initial offer may start at $230,000. With a fair market value of $275,000 (based on an all fixed up value), means that with the needed renovations, that the as-is value is about $245,000. Therefore, your target price for this property is between $240,000 and $245,000. Please note that all properties are unique and all properties can cashflow depending on how you make the deal and how much you can spend to get the property. How motivated the sellers are will determine how much of a discount you can attempt to get. As you get more experienced, you will get a feel as to when you can push for more and when you cannot and what you think the seller will accept.

Now that you know where your bottom line is and where you would like to start, discuss with your real estate agent why you have your numbers and what your bottom figure is. This also is the time where you'll need to put in your clauses which you have discussed with your lawyer. You have the right to put as many conditions that you would like on the offer. However, the more conditions you have, the less likely the seller will entertain your offer. The more conditions that you have will give the sellers the impression that you are a very difficult buyer and possibly not very serious about buying.

Clauses: No. 2, No. 3 and No. 4 Contingencies

There are three must have clauses that you should include as a minimum in all your offers:

> 1. Subject to Lawyer/Partner Approval
> 2. Subject to Inspection
> 3. Subject to Financing

Subject to Lawyer/Partner Approval

The first clause is your *"get out of jail free"* card. This condition gives you the opportunity to break the contract for basically any reason. If the deal just doesn't seem right to you, you always can say that your lawyers or partners didn't recommend that you go through with the deal and that they disapproved it. Even though you have this clause, do not over use this as you will start to lose the trust and support of your real estate agent. Remember that for you to have a strong team you must all be adding value to each other. If you are constantly utilizing the partners' approval clause because you just didn't 'feel' right, then you soon will lose your real estate agent who has been working very hard for you.

Subject to Inspection

The second and third clauses are very common and are usually included in contracts regardless. The subject to inspection basically gives you the opportunity to get out of the deal if the inspection comes up with issues that you did not anticipate during the viewing and your analysis. You can have your contractors give you their thoughts and if your original estimate for renovations was too low, this would be a good opportunity to exit the deal using this clause or renegotiate a new purchase price.

Subject to Financing

Finally, the subject to financing clause allows you to exit the deal if the financing condition that you can arrange for does not meet your requirements. For example, if you did your analysis based on a 20 percent down payment and it turns out that the best lender you can find is asking for 30 percent, then this is a good time to exit with this clause if the deal no longer makes sense. It also can be said for the rate of your mortgage, the amortization period and the conditions that were laid out with your money lender.

With these three clauses, you have the opportunity to get out of your deal, if accepted, within a previously agreed amount of days with the seller. You can see that a lot of the fear and risk is mitigated when these three clauses are used. Do not forget that the clauses can be used as part of your negotiation. Let's say you are very confident with the condition of the property and already have a money partner in place, you may not need such a long condition lift date. If the seller is in need of a short condition date and fast close, you may tell them that you can take off the inspection and financing clauses for a discount on the purchase price. With more experience, you will learn to use each aspect of the contract as a negotiation tool.

Importance of Dates

Now that you have your clauses in place, the next step is deciding which dates to lift conditions and take possession.

Condition Date

Date to lift conditions, is as it is stated, the date at which the conditions you have stated need to be lifted if you are to continue with the deal. This is the time period when you will get all your final checks done:

- Arranging for financing
- Finding an inspector
- Getting an appraisal done if needed

- Confirming required renovations and required costs
- Arranging the paperwork for your joint venture partners
- Arrange paperwork with or finding tenants

Due to the fact that there is a lot of things that need to be done, ideally you would like this date to be as far out from the offer accepting date as possible. However once the offer is accepted the seller is no longer allowed to sell the property to anyone else, meaning during the condition date period, the property is at a standstill. So if you decide not to lift conditions then the seller would have lost valuable showing opportunities. Therefore, when asking for a condition lift date, be respectful of the seller's time. A respectable amount of time is 10 business days.

A tip that we would recommend is that you request right on the offer the following: "*10 business days after the acceptance of the offer.*" If an actual date is written, you may need to change it numerous times due to the unknown time needed for negotiations to take place and when the offer will actually get accepted. Some selling agents may not accept this request, however it doesn't hurt to ask.

Keep in mind that as long as you are serious about your offer and you have been using the time to get everything together, most sellers are reasonable so that if an extension is needed to lift conditions an addendum can be done. Depending on the situation of the seller, there are instances where a condition date of 30 days after acceptance date has been set. Further details as to what you need to do during this time will be discussed in the next chapter. If the seller is unwilling to grant you 10 business days ask for as much as you can. You may want to warn the seller that it may take more time for you to arrange the inspection and the lenders to qualify you for the property in that short period of time, so that if an extension is needed that they would not be surprised.

Possession Date

Possession date is the date when you receive the keys to the property and you now are the owner of the property. You would usually like to have this date as far out as possible. A few days before the possession date is when you will need to have the remainder of your down payment.

However, if you have tenants and financing already in place, you may want possession sooner to accommodate your tenant's needs.

After you lift conditions and the offer is accepted, the property is yours and you are contractually bounded to the deal. Therefore, the longer you have for possession date the better. This will give you more time to find tenants, money partners, investors or time to arrange for funding, so that by the time you do take possession you will have everything in place, maximizing your returns. All this can be done while the property is safely secured and without you needing to pay for it! A respectable time for a possession date is approximately 30 days after the date of acceptance. Depending on the situation of the seller there are instances where a possession date of three months after acceptance date has been set.

Now that you see the importance of the condition and possession dates keep in mind that you can use these dates as part of your negotiations. The seller may require a very short condition lift date, therefore, compensate for your request to get an additional discount. Likewise, you may consider paying more for the property to get a much longer possession date.

Deposits, Down Payments and Purchase Price

To make the contract a legal document, an initial deposit will be needed. This amount will be returned to you if the deal doesn't happen. Contrastingly, this amount will go toward your down payment on the property if the deal is accepted. It is common practice to have the initial deposit at $5,000. Remember the more money you keep for the longer period of time the better. Therefore, we recommend that you offer an initial deposit of $1,000. If this is rejected, you may consider an initial deposit of $1,000 and another $1,500 upon the acceptance of the offer. Like the dates and clauses, this is another area that can be negotiated. How much potential the property has may determine how much you will put down as a deposit. Some agents may fill in all the other numbers such as the financing amount, the down payment amount and remaining down payment amount. To keep things simple and to reduce paper work due to negotiating, only the initial deposit and the final purchase price is needed at this point and the rest can be filled in during final acceptance when the purchase price has been verbally agreed. Keep in mind that the initial deposit will be required within 72 hours after acceptance of the offer. This is to give the seller some security as you do your due diligence before lifting conditions (discussed in the following chapters). If you wanted to put in multiple offers, keeping the initial deposit low will allow you to put in more offers.

The final part of the offer is the purchase price of the property. The purchase price actually consists of a few numbers. Most importantly, is the purchase price that you would like to offer. This will be the price you have decided to start with, in our example, $260,000. You can fully expect that the seller will reject this offer. This is a good thing! If they actually accepted your offer, it means you might have offered too much. Therefore, if the offer is accepted, be especially careful with your checks to make sure that you didn't forget something. In most cases, the sellers will counter your offer. Depending on what their counter is, will show you how willing the seller is going to come down on their price.

Using our property for example where the asking price is $290,000, our offer is $260,000, and our target is $275,000. If the counter is $280,000, then you know you are able to come back with a counter offer and that the target of $275,000 is within reach. If the counter offer was $288,000 then you know that getting them down to $275,000 will be very difficult or not realistic. A good habit to have is to stay away from round looking numbers. This means that instead of countering their $288,000 with $270,000, counter with $271,250 or $269,780. Use the visual power of numbers to your advantage and give a little more to get the grand prize.

"Lose the battles to win the war."

A counter offer of $272,000 is more powerful than $270,000. Your final offer is about $275,000. Giving a little more during negotiation phase may actually get them to accept a lower offer than you originally thought. Also another good habit to have is to mirror the seller's movements. If they come down $10,000 you can go up $8,000 to $12,000. Likewise, if they only come down $1,000, you can try $2,000. Of course, this all depends on how great a deal you are getting and how much cashflow you can potentially get. For example, if the seller only came down to $288,000 from $290,000 and told you that's their final offer, but you know you can still cashflow about $500 a month you may be willing to give your final offer of $280,000 as a take it or leave it situation. You might be surprised with a counter offer of $285,000. Therefore, as you can see, the purchase price can take some time to reach. As long as you keep your emotions from the deal and have the numbers do the talking, you will not accept a deal that you didn't want. If the deal is accepted, GREAT! If not, on to the next property. Remember that all changes must be initialed by both the sellers and buyers.

Action Cures Fear

Now that you have everything completed, the offer is ready to be submitted. At first, this process can be very overwhelming. Looking back, putting in our first offer was the scariest. At the time, we were looking at a condo that was listed for $130,000 and our offer was for $90,000 hoping to get the unit for $110,000. We were scared out of our minds. The funny thing was we were actually scared of what we are going to do if our initial offer was accepted! In retrospect, if it was accepted, it would have been a great deal. If it turned out to be a bad deal, we still had clauses to leave the deal. So looking back at that moment, we realize now that there was nothing to fear. In the end, the seller only reduced their price by $2,000 showing that we were just too far apart. We also found out that the seller had a few other units and that they were investors living in another city. Clearly, they were not in need to sell the property and were waiting for what they wanted.

Always get your real estate agent to ask questions to find out more about the seller's situation. After we let the unit go, we went through hundreds of other properties and offers. Finally, we got our first property and we built our portfolio from there. The thing we had to remember is that regardless of how many offers were rejected, we had to be persistent. With each offer we made, the more natural it felt. With each offer that was rejected, the more we learned about negotiating, and with each property we assessed, the easier it was to make offers. The more we did, the more we were able to anticipate what would happen, hence reducing our risk of getting a bad property or opportunity. Anything that is successful is a result of persistence. Ever wonder why the soft drink 7-Up is called 7-Up? The first six tries failed, but with each try, they changed the combination until they found the magical formula with the seventh trial. So don't give up and continue to look at properties and make offers! The more offers you make, the chances of you getting a deal gets higher which will allow you to set up a property so you can Make More and Work Less with Cashflow.

There is a fine balancing act in play during negotiations. Make sure that all parties come out as winners.

The following is a sample of a purchase contract. Note that each modification and page must be initialed (for easier viewing, go to www.makemoreworklessbook.com/cashflow).

RESIDENTIAL REAL ESTATE PURCHASE CONTRACT

This Residential Purchase Contract (the "Contract") is between

THE SELLER	and	THE BUYER

Name_____ Name Assurance Real Estate Acquisitions_____

Name_____ Name_____

1. THE PROPERTY

1.1 The Property is the Land, Buildings, Attached Goods (unless excluded) and included Unattached Goods located at (municipal address):_____

1.2 The legal description of the Property is:

Plan_____ Block_____ Lot_____ Other_____

1.3 No Unattached Goods (chattels) except for:

Dryer, Refrigerator, Refrigerators-Two, Stoves-Two, Stove-Electric, Washer

1.4 All Attached Goods (fixtures) except for:

1.5 Unless otherwise agreed in writing, title will be free and clear of all encumbrances, registrations and obligations except the following:

(a) those implied by law;

(b) non-financial obligations now on title such as easements, utility rights-of-way, covenants and conditions that are normally found registered against property of this nature and which do not affect the saleability of the Property;

(c) homeowner association caveats, encumbrances and similar registrations; and

(d) those items which the Buyer agreed to assume in this Contract.

2. THE TRANSACTION

2.1 The Buyer and the Seller agree to act cooperatively, reasonably, diligently and in good faith.

2.2 The Buyer hereby offers to purchase the Property for the Purchase Price specified and allocated below:

$ 2,000.00 _____ Initial Deposit

$ _____ Additional Deposit

$ _____ Assumption of Mortgage
(approximate principal balance as per attached Financing Schedule)

$ _____

$ 184,000.00 _____ New Financing

$ _____ Seller Financing (as per attached Financing Schedule)

$ _____ Other Value

$ 44,000.00 _____ Balance Owing (subject to adjustments)

$ 230,000.00 _____ **Purchase Price**

Unless otherwise agreed in writing, the Purchase Price includes any applicable Goods and Services Tax (GST).

2.3 Other than the Deposits, the Buyer shall pay the Purchase Price by lawyer's trust cheque, bank draft or other agreed value.

_____ Seller's Initials _____ Buyer's Initials   Page 1 of 6

Figure: 8-1 – Sample Offer to Purchase page 1
(courtesy of Josh Tesolin – Realtor & Alberta Real Estate Association)
NOTE:
1. Company name add "and/or assignee"
2. Initial deposit of $2,000
3. Starting offer

3. DEPOSITS

3.1 All Deposits shall be delivered in trust to _____

Unless otherwise agreed in writing, the Initial Deposit shall accompany the offer: _____

3.2 The Initial Deposit shall be deposited no later than the third Business Day following the day that Final Signing occurred (as per clause 15.1). Additional Deposits shall be deposited no later than the third Business Day following the day the Additional Deposit is received by the brokerage.

3.3 Any Additional Deposits shall be delivered as follows: _____

3.4 Unless otherwise agreed in writing, no interest on the Deposits shall be paid to the Seller or the Buyer _____

3.5 The Deposits shall be held in trust for both the Seller and the Buyer and shall be:

(a) applied against the Commission and paid directly out of trust to the brokerage(s) when the Commission is earned in accordance with the terms of the Listing Contract;

(b) refunded forthwith to the Buyer if this offer is not accepted;

(c) refunded forthwith to the Buyer upon the Buyer's cheque clearing the brokerage's trust account if a condition is not satisfied or waived (as per clauses 8.5 and 8.6) or the Seller fails to perform this Contract; and

(d) forfeited to the Seller if this offer is accepted and all conditions are satisfied or waived and the Buyer fails to perform this Contract.

3.6 The brokerage holding the Deposits is further directed and authorized to pay that portion of the Deposits exceeding the Commission in trust to the Seller's lawyer no later than two (2) Business Days prior to the Completion Day.

3.7 If there is a dispute between the Seller and the Buyer as to entitlement to the Deposits then:

(a) the brokerage holding the Deposits shall review the circumstances, determine entitlement and pay the money to the party who is entitled to the Deposits;

(b) if no reasonable conclusion can be made in regard to (a) above, the brokerage shall notify the parties to the Contract in writing and shall pay the money into a lawyer's trust account;

(c) the parties agree to allow the lawyer or the brokerage to deduct from the Deposits a reasonable fee and costs incurred for dealing with the Deposits;

(d) a brokerage and/or lawyer acting in good faith under this clause shall not be liable to either party for any damages associated with the handling of the Deposits, except as arising from the negligence of the brokerage or lawyer.

3.8 In the event that the brokerage holding the trust funds ceases to be licensed in real estate, the Buyer and Seller agree to allow the trust funds to be transferred to the brokerage representing the other party.

4. CLOSING

4.1 Unless otherwise agreed in writing, this Contract will be completed, the Purchase Price will be fully paid and vacant possession will be available by 12 noon on the 29 day of July , 2012 (the "Completion Day"), subject to the rights of the existing tenants, if any.

4.2 When the Buyer obtains possession, the Property will be in substantially the same condition as it was in when this Contract was accepted.

4.3 Items which are normally adjusted for, such as real estate property taxes, amortized local improvement levies, utilities, rents, security deposits, statutory interest on security deposits, mortgage interest and homeowner association fees, will be assumed by the Buyer and will be adjusted as of 24:00 hours on the Completion Day.

4.4 The Seller or the Seller's lawyer will deliver normal closing documents including, where applicable, a real property report pursuant to clause 4.11, to the Buyer or the Buyer's lawyer upon reasonable conditions consistent with the terms of this Contract. The Buyer or the Buyer's lawyer must have an opportunity to review the real property report, where applicable, prior to submitting the transfer documents to the Land Titles Office and a reasonable period of time before the Completion Day to confirm registration of documents at the Land Titles Office and to obtain the advance of proceeds for any New Financing and Other Value.

4.5 If the Seller fails to deliver the closing documents according to clause 4.4, then payment of the Purchase Price and late interest will be postponed until the Buyer has received the closing documents and has a reasonable period of time to register them and to obtain the advance of proceeds for any New Financing and Other Value. Notwithstanding the foregoing, if the Buyer is otherwise ready, willing and able to close in accordance with this Contract and desires to take possession of the Property, then the Seller shall give the Buyer possession upon reasonable terms which will include the payment of late interest only on the amount of mortgage being obtained by the Buyer, if any, at the interest rate of such mortgage.

4.6 In circumstances where the Seller has complied with clause 4.4 but the Buyer is not able to close in accordance with this Contract, then the Seller may, but is not obligated to, accept late payment of the Purchase Price and give the Buyer possession upon reasonable terms. If the Seller agrees in writing to accept late payment of the Purchase Price under this clause then, whether or not possession is granted, the Buyer will pay late interest at the prime lending rate of the Province of Alberta Treasury Branches at the Completion Day plus 3% calculated daily from and including the Completion Day to (but excluding) the day the Seller is paid in full. Payment received after noon on any day will be payment as of the next Business Day.

4.7 The Seller's lawyer may use the Purchase Price to pay out all mortgages, registrations and other financial obligations that are the Seller's obligation to pay or discharge. Within a reasonable period of time after the Completion Day, the Seller's lawyer will provide the Buyer's lawyer with evidence of all discharges including, where required, a certified copy of the certificate of title.

Figure: 8-2 – Sample Offer to Purchase page 2
(courtesy of Josh Tesolin – Realtor & Alberta Real Estate Association)

NOTE:

1. Possession date in Section 4.1
2. Initial deposit is required with 72 hours of acceptance

4.8	The Seller will pay the costs to prepare the closing documents; to prepare, register and discharge any Seller's caveat based on this Contract; and to provide the documents described in clause 4.11.
4.9	The Buyer will pay the costs to prepare, register and discharge any Buyer's caveat based on this Contract; and to register the transfer of land.
4.10	If the Property is rented and the Buyer is not assuming the tenancy, then the Seller is responsible for all costs related to ending the tenancy and to giving vacant possession to the Buyer.
4.11	As part of the normal closing documents, the Seller will provide the Buyer, regarding the matters described in clause 6.1, a real property report reflecting the current state of improvement on the Property, according to the Alberta Land Surveyors' Manual of Standard Practice, with evidence of municipal compliance or non-conformance. This obligation will not apply to any transaction where there are no structures on the land.
4.12	Notwithstanding the closing provisions in this Contract, the parties instruct their lawyers to follow, if appropriate, the Law Society of Alberta Conveyancing Protocol in the closing of this transaction.

5. INSURANCE

5.1	The risk of loss or damage to the Property shall lie with the Seller until the Purchase Price is paid according to the terms of this Contract. If loss or damage to the Property occurs before the Seller is paid the Purchase Price, then any insurance proceeds shall be held in trust for the Buyer and the Seller according to their interests in the Property.

6. REPRESENTATIONS AND WARRANTIES

6.1	The Seller represents and warrants to the Buyer that:

(a) the Seller has the legal right to sell the Property;

(b) the Attached Goods and Included Unattached Goods are in normal working order and are free and clear of all encumbrances;

(c) the Seller is not a non-resident of Canada for the purposes of the *Income Tax Act* (Canada);

(d) the current use of the Land and Buildings complies with the existing municipal land use bylaw;

(e) the Buildings and other improvements on the Land are not placed partly or wholly on any easement or utility right-of-way and are entirely on the Land and do not encroach on neighbouring lands, except where an encroachment agreement is registered on title, or in the case of an encroachment into municipal lands or a right-of-way, the municipality has endorsed encroachment approval directly on the real property report;

(f) the location of Buildings and other improvements on the Land complies with all relevant municipal bylaws, regulations or relaxations granted by the appropriate municipality prior to the Completion Day, or the Buildings and other improvements on the Land are "non-conforming buildings" as that term is defined in the *Municipal Government Act* (Alberta);

(g) the current use of the Land and Buildings and the location of the Buildings and other improvements on the Land comply with any restrictive covenant on title;

(h) except as otherwise disclosed, the Seller is not aware of any defects that are not visible and that may render the Property dangerous or potentially dangerous to occupants or unfit for habitation.

6.2	All of the warranties contained in this Contract and any attached Schedules are made as of and will be true at the Completion Day, unless otherwise agreed in writing.
6.3	The representations and warranties in this Contract may be enforced after the Completion Day, provided that any legal action is commenced within the time limits prescribed by the *Limitations Act* (Alberta).
6.4	The Seller and the Buyer each acknowledge that, except as otherwise described in this Contract, there are no other warranties, representations or collateral agreements made by or with the other party, the Seller's brokerage and the Buyer's brokerage about the Property, any neighbouring lands, and this transaction, including any warranty, representation or collateral agreement relating to the size/measurements of the Land and Buildings or the existence or non-existence of any environmental condition or problem.

7. ADDITIONAL TERMS

7.1	All time periods, deadlines and dates in this Contract shall be strictly followed and enforced. All times will be Alberta time unless otherwise stated.
7.2	This Contract is for the benefit of and shall be binding upon the heirs, executors, administrators and assigns of the individual parties and the successors and assigns of corporate parties.
7.3	All changes of number and gender shall be made where required.
7.4	This Contract will be governed by the laws of the Province of Alberta. The parties submit to the exclusive jurisdiction of the Courts in the Province of Alberta regarding any dispute that may arise out of this transaction.
7.5	In addition to any Schedules required in Section 8, the following Schedules form part of this Contract: ☐ Financing Schedule ☐ Addendum ☐ Property Schedule
7.6	Additional terms of sale (if any):

Seller's Initials _____ Buyer's Initials _____ Page 3 of 6

Figure: 8-3 – Sample Offer to Purchase page 3
(courtesy of Josh Tesolin – Realtor & Alberta Real Estate Association)

164

8.	CONDITIONS

8.1 The Buyer's Conditions are:

(a) **Financing Condition**

This Contract is subject to the Buyer securing New Financing as follows:

- as per clause 2.2 (plus applicable mortgage insurance fee, if any)
- interest rate not to exceed _____ percent a year calculated semi-annually not in advance
- a term of not less than _____ years

Monthly payment of principal and interest not to exceed $ _____ (including mortgage insurance fee, if applicable) for an amortization of 25 years.

Before 9 p.m. on _within 10 business days of final acceptance_ _____ (the "Condition Day").

The Buyer will pay for all costs associated with the New Financing.

(b) **Property Inspection Condition**

This Contract is subject to the Buyer's approval of a property inspection.

Before 9 p.m. on _within 10 business days of final acceptance_ _____ (the "Condition Day").

A Property Inspection Schedule is attached to and forms part of the Contract. ☐ Yes ☑ No

(c) **Sale of Buyer's Home Condition**

This Contract is subject to the sale of the Buyer's home, as per attached Sale of Buyer's Home Schedule. ☐ Yes ☐ No

Before 9 p.m. on _____ (the "Condition Day").

(d) **Additional Buyer's Conditions:**

Subject to financing suitable to the buyer.
Subject to Buyer's Lawyer's/Partner's Approval

Before 9 p.m. on _within 10 business days of final acceptance_ _____ (the "Condition Day").

8.2 The Seller's Conditions are:

Before 9 p.m. on _____ (the "Condition Day").

8.3 If this Contract contemplates an assumption of mortgage, then it is subject to the lender confirming the assumability of the mortgage by the Buyer.

Before 9 p.m. on _____ (the "Condition Day").

This Condition is for the mutual benefit of both the Buyer and the Seller and cannot be waived unilaterally.

8.4 Unless otherwise agreed in writing, the Buyer's Conditions are for the sole benefit of the Buyer and the Seller's Conditions are for the sole benefit of the Seller. The Buyer and Seller must use reasonable efforts to satisfy their respective Conditions.

8.5 The Buyer and the Seller may unilaterally waive or acknowledge satisfaction of their Conditions by giving a written notice to the other party on or before the stated Condition Day. If that notice is not given, then this Contract is ended immediately following that Condition Day.

8.6 Subject to clause 8.4, the Buyer and the Seller may give written notice to the other party on or before the stated Condition Day advising that a Condition will not be waived, has not been satisfied and will not be satisfied on or before the Condition Day. If that notice is given, then this Contract is ended upon the giving of that notice.

9.	REMEDIES/DISPUTES

9.1 If the Seller or the Buyer fails or refuses to complete this Contract according to its terms, then the other party may pursue all available remedies. The Seller's remedies include keeping the Deposits and claiming additional damages. Both the Seller and the Buyer can claim reasonable costs including legal fees and disbursements on a solicitor/client full indemnity basis.

9.2 If the Seller must restore title to the Property, enforce a lien against the Property or regain possession of the Property due to the Buyer's default, then the Buyer will pay the Seller's reasonable costs including legal fees and disbursements on a solicitor/client full indemnity basis.

10.	ADVICE/DISCLOSURE

10.1 This Contract is intended to create binding legal obligations. The Seller and the Buyer should read this Contract carefully and are encouraged to obtain legal advice before signing.

10.2 Any representations as to the measurements of the Buildings are only approximations and may not be accurate. The Buyer may wish to obtain an independent property inspection and verify the measurements of the Land and Buildings.

_____ Seller's Initials _____ Buyer's Initials   Page 4 of 6

Figure: 8-4 – Sample Offer to Purchase page 4
(courtesy of Josh Tesolin – Realtor & Alberta Real Estate Association)
NOTE:

1. Subject to financing condition
2. Subject to inspection
3. Subject to lawyer and partner approval
4. Condition date

10.3 Unless there is written consent for alternate representation, the Seller's brokerage represents the Seller as Seller's Agent and does not have a fiduciary relationship with the Buyer, and the Buyer's brokerage represents the Buyer as Buyer's Agent and does not have a fiduciary relationship with the Seller.

10.4 The Seller and the Seller's brokerage have signed a Listing Contract. The Seller directs the Seller's lawyer to honour the terms of the Listing Contract and in particular to close the transaction according to the irrevocable assignment of the Purchase Price contained in the Listing Contract.

10.5 The Buyer and Seller agree that the sale and other related information regarding this transaction may be retained and disclosed by the brokerage and/or the real estate boards(s) as required for closing and for reporting, appraisal and statistical purposes.

10.6 This Contract may be signed and sent by fax and this procedure will be as effective as signing and delivering an original copy.

10.7 Dower consent may be required for this Purchase Contract to be binding if title is in only one name and the registered owner is legally married.

11. DEFINITIONS

11.1 In this Contract:

(a) *Business Day* means a day when the Land Titles Office is open for business.

(b) *Buyer's Agent* means the licensed brokerage (including its broker, all associate brokers and associates) that represents the Buyer.

(c) *Commission* means the sum owing from the Seller for services rendered under the Listing Contract plus GST.

(d) *Completion Day* is the day described in clause 4.1.

(e) *Deposits* mean the Initial Deposit plus all Additional Deposits.

(f) *Listing Contract* means any written service or commission agreement obligating the Seller to pay remuneration.

(g) *Notice* means any notice referred to in this Contract and includes communication of the acceptance of an offer to purchase.

(h) *Seller's Agent* means the licensed brokerage (including its broker, all associate brokers and associates) that represents the Seller.

(i) *Unless otherwise agreed in writing* means either changes made to the terms of this Contract that are agreed to by both the Seller and the Buyer, or a written agreement by letter or otherwise between the Seller or the Seller's lawyer and the Buyer or the Buyer's lawyer.

12. REPRESENTATIVES/NOTICE

12.1 As long as the Representative information in 12.2 is completed, the identified Representatives are authorized to send and receive any Notice on behalf of their respective clients.

12.2 For the purposes of giving and receiving any Notice, the communication must be in writing and

(a) delivered in person to the other party or its Representative, or

(b) delivered (or faxed) to an address (or fax number) specified below.

Note: The Representative information must be completed in full by the Buyer's Agent at the offer stage prior to the Contract being signed in order to permit communication on the Representatives.

Seller's Information:
Seller's Address _____
_____ Phone _____ Fax _____
(postal code)

Seller's Representative:
_____
Broker, associate broker or associate registered to the brokerage
Brokerage Name _____
Address _____
Representative's Phone _____ Representative's Fax _____

Buyer's Information:
Buyer's Address _____
_____ Phone _____ Fax _____
(postal code)

Buyer's Representative:
_____
Broker, associate broker or associate registered to the brokerage
Brokerage Name _____
Address _____
Representative's Phone _____ Representative's Fax _____

_____ Seller's Initials _____ Buyer's Initials   Page 5 of 6

Figure: 8-5 – Sample Offer to Purchase page 5
(courtesy of Josh Tesolin – Realtor & Alberta Real Estate Association)

13. OFFER

13.1 The Buyer offers to buy the Property for the Purchase Price according to the terms of this Contract.

13.2 This offer/counter offer shall be open for acceptance in writing until _____.m. on _____, 20_____.

SIGNED AND DATED at Edmonton _____, Alberta at _____ p.m. on June 28, _____, 2012

Signature of Buyer	Signature of Witness
Assurance Real Estate Acquisitions	
Print Name of Buyer	Print Name of Witness
Signature of Buyer	Signature of Witness
Print Name of Buyer	Print Name of Witness

14. ACCEPTANCE

14.1 The Seller accepts the Buyer's offer and agrees to sell the Property for the Purchase Price according to the terms of this Contract.

SIGNED AND DATED at _____, Alberta at _____.m. on _____, 20_____.

Signature of Seller	Signature of Witness
Print Name of Seller	Print Name of Witness
Signature of Seller	Signature of Witness
Print Name of Seller	Print Name of Witness

15. FINAL SIGNING

15.1 Final Signing of this Contract occurred at _____.m. on _____, 20_____.
Initials of the person(s) who signed last _____

CONVEYANCING

Seller's Lawyer _____

Lawyer's Address _____
(postal code)

Lawyer's Phone _____ Fax _____

Buyer's Lawyer _____

Lawyer's Address _____
(postal code)

Lawyer's Phone _____ Fax _____

Page 6 of 6

Figure: 8-6 – Sample Offer to Purchase page 6
(courtesy of Josh Tesolin – Realtor & Alberta Real Estate Association)

MAKE MORE WORK LESS with CASHFLOW

Chapter 8 – Have No Fears: Make Great Offers

Your present circumstances don't determine where you can go; they merely determine where you start.

- Nido Qubein -

Assurance Keys to Your Success

- The 80-20 rule – be persistent

- Company Name and/or Assignee

- Assess your starting point and read your seller to determine motivation and negotiation effort

- Clauses: Subject to lawyer/partner approval
    Subject to inspection
    Subject to financing

- Condition date: 10 or more business days

- Possession date: 30 days after acceptance

- Keep as much money as you can in your hands
    Have initial deposit start at $1,000

- Lose the battle to win the war

- Don't give up, find the winning formula

Chapter - 9 -

Due Diligence Part I:
Trust But Verify

Diligence is the mother of good luck.

- Benjamin Franklin -

"It got accepted! It got accepted! Oh no! Oh no! What do we do now?" John and Melissa said with excitement. We chuckled and looked over their offer contract and reviewed their numbers. Indeed the property was a good opportunity and worth acquiring. We told them to calm down and that everything will be fine. We will just need to work fast and get everything sorted out to make sure we are able to lift conditions.

You got a phone call or a text message from your real estate agent and you hear the magic words "they accepted the offer!" AWESOME! After looking at tons of properties, running a mind-blowing amount of numbers and went through an exciting period of negotiations your offer is accepted! You have just crossed another barrier or hurdle and most importantly, you have conquered another fear. Now comes the time when you must reassure and confirm that the property is everything you expect it to be and your initial analysis is correct. Remember, the length of your condition period determines how much time you have to get everything in order. The more you have worked with your team members: your mortgage broker, your lawyer, your contractors and real estate agent before the deal will help keep this process running smoothly and calmly.

What to Do

So what will you need to do first? You have a few days, in most cases 10 business days to get everything in order. The best way to organize is to have a checklist developed of all the things that is needed and organize it in order of what needs to be done first. The following are the steps that we follow to assure us that everything is completed:

1. Send purchase contract to mortgage broker
2. Send purchase contract to lawyer
3. Discuss path forward with mortgage broker
4. Supply mortgage broker with updated financial documents: employment letter, paystubs, notice of assessment from previous tax year, proof of funds for down payment and gift letter if need be

5. Contact contractors and renovators to assess the amount of work needed and to give you a quote
6. Study rental market
7. If required by lender, arrange for an appraisal
8. Arrange for inspection
9. Post as rental unit to gauge market
10. Prepare a summary sheet
11. Talk to potential money partners or Joint Venture partners if needed

After the offer is accepted, you can instruct your real estate agent to send all necessary documents, mainly the purchase contract and listing, to your mortgage broker and lawyer. Follow up with your mortgage broker and lawyer to ask what the best plan to move forward is.

With the Mortgage Broker

With the mortgage broker, the following will need to be discussed: rate, term, amortization period, mortgage type, down payment and potential lenders.

Typically, a 20 percent down payment will be needed. However, one can have access to more lenders at better conditions if you were to increase the down payment to 25 percent or 30 percent. This has its advantages as your cashflow will increase and more options are available to you. If you or your money partner would rather the high cashflow, then a higher down payment may be a good option to consider.

Term

The term of the mortgage is typically between three to five years. The strategy you and your mortgage broker discussed will determine which is best for your property. For instance, if you were looking at a buy-fix-and-flip property, a one-year term or shorter may be a good suggestion, but for a long-term cashflow investment, a five-year term may make more sense. The term, type and rate of the mortgage will go hand-in-hand. The shorter the term, the higher the rate. Likewise, if you choose a variable open mortgage, you may get lower rates compared to a fixed-closed mortgage. In general, we would like to go for the lowest rate we can get with minimal payout penalties if exited out early. A good mortgage broker will give you their recommendations and also the pros and cons of different recommended products. Ask them to tell you what your monthly payments will be. Some lenders like to reduce their risk by requiring you to pay mortgage insurance. The amount of this insurance can range depending on the amount of down payment you use. We would like to stress that we are not experts in the world of mortgages and therefore it is very important for you to have a great broker that understands investing in real estate so that you can ask questions and get the best product for your property.

Side note: we recommend that you DO NOT sign for mortgage insurance with the lender. This is the type of insurance where if anything goes wrong and you are unable to pay the mortgage, the mortgage will be paid. In plain view, this sounds great and perfect for your family's security. However, if you look in the fine print, it is very rare for someone to actually qualify for that insurance.

Chances are great, you will be paying a monthly charge for the insurance (which depreciates over time as you pay the mortgage down) to find out that when you need it, you don't qualify. There are many better options out there for your family's security. Mortgage insurance is NOT one of them (life insurance would be a better option – consult with your insurance broker).

Amortization Period

The amortization period is how long you can take to pay off the mortgage. Traditionally, people want to pay off their mortgage as soon as possible. However, if you were to think like an investor, you would like to use other people's money as long as possible. This is the power of leverage. As long as your cashflow remains where you are happy, you don't need to pay off the loan. By doing so, it will allow you to use other capital on other investments. Therefore, having said that, we would like to get amortization periods to be as long as we can, anywhere from 25 to 40 years! By spreading the payout period further into the future, you will actually reduce your monthly payment and increase your cashflow. Generally, a 25-year period is what most lenders will allow.

Money Lenders

If you have a money lender/partner in place, then everything that you would be discussing with your mortgage broker will be the same as what you would discuss with your money lender. You will find that with private money there will be a lot more flexibility but the rates will be higher. Most private money lenders are short-term lenders and therefore, are great for locking properties that require quick closes. We recommend that even though you have private money that you still consult with your mortgage broker so that you venture all options and can pick the one best for you. A good broker will be open to hear what your private money conditions are and will give you their thoughts on it as well without being biased. Having private money allows you to build that relationship and the loan will not affect your credit score (credit score is what traditional lenders use to determine your qualifying ability). Regardless, having discussions with your private money lender and mortgage broker is very important at this stage.

For your mortgage broker to find you the best lender for your strategy, you will need to provide them with either your financial information or that of your joint venture partner, depending on who you have decided to be on title. The following will be what is needed:

- Application form of your assets and liabilities if you haven't done one already – see sample from before
- Employment letter that proves current employment, for how long and for what income
- Recent paystubs to prove income
- Recent notice of assessment
- Proof of down payment
- Current rental leases
- Current mortgages
- Gift letter – if needed from family member - basically claiming that a certain amount of money is given to the purchaser and that repayment is not required

With regards to gift letters please note that these can only be done if the person giving you the gift is a family member. If your joint venture partners are the ones going on title then the gift will need to come from their family member.

After all the necessary documents have been given to your mortgage broker you can now wait to see when the mortgage is approved and when you can arrange to have it signed.

The process of getting approval for a mortgage will take the most time and therefore, it is recommended that this is the first thing you do. The final mortgage doesn't need to be in place until the possession date; however, one would like to know that at the very least they have verbal confirmation that they are approved for the mortgage before lifting conditions. Therefore, until your mortgage broker tells you that you have a mortgage verbally in place and that only formal paper work needs to be done, DO NOT lift conditions. If the response to getting approval is not looking good and all other lender options have been considered then it is time to exercise the financing clause, not lift the condition and exit the deal. If your mortgage broker requires more time for an approval and that all the documents have been submitted, then ask your real estate agent to ask for an extension. In general, as long as the seller sees that you are doing your best to get your financing in place, they will most likely give you an extension, unless they have backup offers accepted, in which case, you may want to discuss with your mortgage broker to assess the risks of lifting conditions and the chances of getting a suitable mortgage for the property in time for possession.

Lawyer

How you set up this property will determine what needs to be discussed with your lawyer. For the first time, or if you see a nonstandard purchase contract, you may want your lawyer to review the contract for anything unusual and have him or her explain the terms of the contract with you. This will give you an idea of what you are signing. In general, most contracts are very similar and therefore, after having your lawyer go through it with you once, you should be OK with reviewing future purchase contracts, unless something is concerning you. If you have a joint venture partner, then this also is the time to have your lawyer start drafting a joint venture agreement between all parties involved. As long as the joint venture partner is someone that you will do projects with, getting a joint venture agreement at this time is recommended. This is because even if the said property does not go though, you always can use the joint venture agreement on another project with minor changes, therefore reducing the time for preparation. Prior to having your lawyer draft the agreement, you may want to have the terms agreed upon with your joint venture partner. Ask your lawyer what other terms or conditions they would recommend that you might be missing. Remember that your lawyers are supposed to have your best interest in mind, so make sure you have them explain to you the terms of the agreement even if you and your joint venture partner came up with it.

It is good practice to give your lawyer a heads up and that if all goes well then they will need to have the necessary papers for you to sign prior to possession date. This will be arranged when you have lifted all conditions and the final acceptance is signed.

Reconfirm your Numbers:
Consult with your Contractor and Coach

Now that you have your mortgage broker and lawyer up to speed with your property, you will need to confirm your numbers and make sure that the property is the investment that you expect it to be. Give your contractors a call and arrange a time for them and your real estate agent to meet at the property. If you have built your relationships well, having a few different contractors there will be fine. This is so you can use your time efficiently, respect the real estate agent's time and also create competition among the contractors. You want a quote for the required and requested renovations for your property and therefore, a competitive yet fair quote is very important. You want the contractors to know that you will have future projects and that you are a fair partner. Have your contractors give broken down quotes, separating the labor cost, the material cost, the cabinets, the floor, paint, etc. This will allow you to compare quotes and also allow you to pick and choose what renovations will be necessary, which will be most beneficial and which will be the best quality option. During their assessment of the property, follow them around and ask questions such as:

- What do you recommend?
- Where do you get your material from?
- How much time will this take?
- Have you done something like this before?

- What would you do to make this look good yet be very cost-efficient?

The answers to these questions will allow you to assess the experience, the creativity and the personality of the contractor.

After all the quotes are done, study the numbers and determine a reasonable and conservative number for renovations. Compare this number with the original estimate that you have done. Were you close? Are the numbers very different? If the results are a lot higher than you expected, you may want to consider renegotiating the purchase price or exercise your inspection clause. You never know what the sellers are willing to do.

For instance, at one property that we were considering, it turns out that upgrading the electrical would have cost us an additional $4,000 to $8,000. After telling the seller that we will not lift conditions due to the electrical and will pass on the deal, the seller was willing to work with us and came up with half the electrical upgrade cost. At the end of the day, you are the one purchasing the property, if the numbers do not work to your expectations you have the right to exit the contract. Remember do not get emotionally attached to the deal!

Appraisal

Now all is ready except for two more items: an appraisal and an inspection. An appraisal may or may not be necessary. It is usually dependent on the lender. Some lenders like to have an appraisal done so that they are comfortable with what they are lending on and that the value of the property is actually the value that you are claiming it to be. Now there are multiple products out there that will lend on an after repair value or an appraised value plus potential renovations cost, but these will need to be discussed with your mortgage broker. Having an appraisal done also is beneficial to you as well, it will either assure you that you have gotten the property at a good price or open it up for re-negotiation if the price is a lot lower. An appraiser will most likely be doing their assessment on the property very similar to what you have done while determining the worth of the property. Depending on which role you are playing will determine whether you want the appraisal to come up higher or lower than your purchase price. In this case, we would like to have the appraisal come in higher so that:

- Proof that you did a good job negotiating to get the price you did
- Renegotiate with the lender for more funds
- Give the lender a peace of mind to approve the loan to you.

In what cases would you want the appraisal to come in lower?

1.   You believe that you can get the property even lower and needed something to get back to the negotiating table
2.   You were the lender and wanted to lend on a lower amount

It is in your best interest to have this scheduled as soon as possible for a date as late as possible to your conditions lift date since you will likely have to pay for the appraisal. Just in case you find reasons to exit the deal, you don't want to have paid for an appraisal and not go through with the deal.

Inspection

The last item that you will need to have completed before you lift conditions is to have an inspection. Of the tasks that you need to do, an inspection may be one of the most important items that must be done. A good inspector will be able to assure you that the property is structurally sound, is safe for living and highlight improvements needed in the short term. Like an appraisal, it is recommended that you schedule an inspector as soon as you can, for a date as late as possible to your conditions lift date. With a price tag for the inspection, you definitely do not want to pay to have an inspection done at the beginning only to find out that your financing didn't come through or the renovation cost is so high that you need to let the deal go. So, like the appraisal, schedule the inspection to be done on the same day as the appraisal. This has its benefits as well. The appraiser and inspector can bounce issues off each other and discuss potential problems should the property have any. When you have your inspector and appraiser there at the property, it is wise to follow them around the property as you would your contractor and ask as many questions you can of them. This is your opportunity to learn the trade. The more you learn the more you will be able to spot certain red flags yourself when you go looking at properties next time. A good inspector and appraiser will be happy to discuss their expertise and occasionally tell you tips and secrets to items that they picked up in their experience. Ask them:

- What they think needs to be fixed or changed?
- How much they think it will cost?
- What would one do to prevent certain issues?
- What would you normally look for if there is a mold issue?
- What would you look for if there was a heating issue?
- Whether the windows are leaking?
- What are you looking for?

Their answers will allow you to rethink your renovation plans, compare their ideas to the quotes you got from your contractors and decide whether you should go back and renegotiate with the seller or pass on the deal. Yes, you may have spent money on the inspection and the appraisal, but it is to your best interest to exit the deal if an inspector finds structural issues that are vital to fix. The last thing you want is to have bought a property and then need to redo the roof after a year and be down $10,000 or down $20,000 due to the need of re-piping the water lines and fixing the water damage to the concrete.

Note: Don't be too surprised to potentially have problems after you take possession of the property. Inspectors and appraisers are not given the right to move items or open holes to inspect the property. Therefore if there are issues hidden from sight then it could be missed. Hence the utmost importance of finding a great inspector, who can see the potential red flags before they happen and without opening up walls.

Depending on how the project is structured between you and your partner, you may ask them for the payments for the lawyer, appraiser and inspector, or pay for them as part of your end of the deal. Always track all the expenses that are needed for all the due diligences to be accomplished.

To Lift or Not to Lift?

At this time, you will have done everything you can to ensure that the property is everything that you expect it to be and that you are either going to lift conditions or not or ask for an extension. Note that conditions can be lifted in any order or any day prior to the condition lift date. In the case where you may need more time for a verbal approval for your financing to come, you may consider lifting the inspection and lawyer conditions and ask for an extension to the financing condition due to the lateness for financing confirmation. If everything is not to your liking then you can either not lift conditions and exit the deal or go back and renegotiate the price due to unforeseen items that was not figured into the price you got from your original analysis. You should ask for the total deduction of the unforeseen amount or to be no less than a 50/50 split. If, in fact, all the numbers, the financing and the inspection come back to your liking, then it is time to lift conditions and sign the final approval of the purchase. At this time, there is no turning back and the deal is final!

Congratulations!

You got the property and everything is working to your liking. Now, you just need to follow up on a few things to ensure that you will close on the property and take possession. The first thing you will need to do is confirm with your mortgage broker that the deal is done and that final funds will be secured prior to the possession date. Likewise you will need to notify your lawyer that purchase contracts will need to be signed and all funds will need to be handled prior to possession date. During this time, it is really just a matter of having your mortgage broker and lawyer get all the documents in order for you to sign. A good lawyer and mortgage broker will be in communication with each other and your real estate agent to make sure all the documents are received and prepped and will explain everything to you when you are scheduled to go see them for final closing.

From the time after conditions have been lifted and your possession date, you will be doing more of what you were doing during the condition period if you do not have the following secured already: a joint venture partner if need be, arranging renovators if need be, to be there right at possession and line up tenants (discussed in next chapter). Other items that you would need to do at this time are the following:

- Arrange to have a separate bank account to keep all financial records simple and clean,
- Ensure that the property taxes will be in order and taken care of,
- Arrange for house insurance and finally arrange for utilities

To find your joint venture partner and tenant is basically what you have been doing this entire time. If you were able get access to the property prior to official possession, then great! Line up the tenants all for one day at 30-minute intervals to save time and to create competition. As for the renovations, if you were able to get approval for renovations to start prior to possession, then that would be best. However, this is not likely as there can be legal ramifications for the seller if anything should happen to the property during this time. Mortgage payments are set up so that they do not start until the next month, therefore, you technically have until the end of the month to have a tenant in place. You can use this to your advantage. Always have your possession dates near the beginning of the month. That way you will have all of the rest of the month to find tenants and have access to show the property without worrying about the month's expenses!

Separate Bank Account

It may not be necessary to open a new account for the property, but it is highly recommended. All funds will go through here and exit here. Mortgage payments, utility payments and property taxes will be recorded through this account. It makes the work for the accountant easier and it gives you easy access to your expenses when need be. When opening this account, remember to ask for the account numbers and the documents needed to approve direct payments for other companies. For example, mortgage payments (may or may not be at the same bank), power and water companies and the city for property taxes. By doing so, you will have fewer headaches and everything will be taken care of themselves.

Property Taxes

Go to the city department that handles the property taxes and make sure to give them the account information needed from the account you have just opened for them to withdraw from when the monthly taxes need to be paid. Have them tell you what amount is to be paid and when it will be deducted. A very good tip here is to build a relationship with one of the property tax experts there. Whenever you have questions about property taxes and when you have future properties, make sure that you are dealing with the same person. You will find that with a relationship built, the process of getting property taxes taken care of will be a lot smoother. Don't be surprised to see the property tax not being withdrawn in the first month or two, as it usually takes some time for it to get set up into the system.

Insurance and Utilities

Finally, call the insurance company and the utility companies to make sure that the property is insured as a rental and has all utilities work on the day of possession (water, power, sewage). Be sure to pass the banking account information needed for direct payment purposes. Always use the same insurance company and have them place all your rental properties under one account (if possible). This is even if the payments are separated from one rental to another, the fact that you have multiple policies may get you a discount overall. Since you are getting insurance for renting your property, the most cost-effective plan will be good enough. Ask what the policy covers and also ask what the difference will be if you added other benefits to your policy. Generally, if the property has a security system, newer roofing, newer furnace, hot water tank, the premiums will be cheaper.

At this stage, you now have a property that you have done all the due diligence in making sure it is the right property for you. Also, at this time, you have a property that is prepped and ready to have tenants in place. Congratulations! You have your cashflow property and now you are ready to watch all your hard work go to work for you. Soon enough, this process of lifting conditions, verifying numbers, setting up the property and taking possession of the property will become second nature that you can do it in your sleep. On top of that, you also will be filled with stories about some of the adventures that you have from inspections and properties that you may have seen.

Strike, Spare and Split Anyone?

One of our favorite stories to share is one we call the "*Bowling Ball House*". Out of town owners rented out the property. The tenants didn't care for the property and basically trashed the place. As we walked into the property, we found something lodged into the wall – a bowling ball! The wall adjacent to the wall with the ball in it, shared a wall with the bathroom. In this wall, there was a bowling ball-sized hole in it, which you can literally be standing in the living room stick you head though the hole and look down at the toilet. With this particular property, we were then able to assess our offer properly and account for all the wreckage left behind by the bowling ball.

You too will accumulate stories of all varieties as you look at more and more properties. Happy property searching, as you build your empire to Make More and Work Less with Cashflow!

The more you do, the more competent you will become. With competence, comes confidence. Confidence leads to success!

Chapter 9 - Due Diligence Part 1
Trust But Verify

*The expectations of life depend upon diligence;
the mechanic that would perfect his work
must first sharpen his tools.*

- Confucius -

Assurance Keys to Your Success

- Prepare a "To Do" checklist

- Discuss with Mortgage Broker on: rate, term, type, amortization and down payment and have all necessary documents ready

- Do not get mortgage insurance, consider life insurance instead

- Have multiple contractors assess work and give quotes

- Book Appraisals and Inspections first for the latest date possible

- Confide with your coach

- Prep for possession: arrange separate bank account, insurance, taxes and utilities

Chapter - 10 -

Due Diligence Part II: Rental Market

Patience and diligence, like faith, remove mountains.

- William Penn -

"OK OK. So now that we are making sure that all the necessary items are taken care of before we lift conditions, is there anything else we need to do? It seems like there is something missing," John asked right before he was about to make the decision to lift conditions on the property.

To have a great cashflowing property, making sure that you have the rental market understood is very important. Although it is not necessary to check that your rent will cover all expenses and provide you cashflow, we believe that it is good practice to figure out all your rental prices and make sure your assumptions on the market are within your assessments, before you lift conditions. If you find that the rental market is not as strong as you thought it would be, you can still decide not to lift conditions and exit the deal.

Study the Rental Market

Now that you have confirmed the renovations cost and have the financing in the works, confirming your cashflow is needed. Study the rental market again to ensure that the rent that you are expecting for the main and basement floors are indeed what you can realistically get. Check the online searches and reconfirm with your property manager again if you feel it is necessary. At this time, you also can post a rental ad in your local rental site, Craig's List, kijiji, or equivalent. There are two major advantages of posting an ad now:

1. You can actually test the interest of renting your property at the prices that you are requesting and

2. You are extending the exposure of your rental to allow for maximum requests.

If you are not getting any responses then chances are, your price point is too high. If you are getting a lot of calls, then your price point is too low. Due to the fact that you do not have access to show the property, all you can tell the potential tenant is that you do not have possession of the property yet but will arrange a time with your real estate agent to see if the seller is willing to allow showings. At this time, you may want to have your real estate agent ask the seller if they can include in the contract the right for you to have access to the property either to show to potential tenants or to do renovations during the time between the lifting of conditions and possession date. Typically, the sellers will allow for access for showings and will do so without the need to add to the contract but will not allow access for renovations. This will reduce the amount of down time that you will have with the property sitting idle and have it ready to cashflow after you take possession. As you are taking calls from interested tenants, remember to take down the potential tenants' name and contact so that when you do have the ability to show the unit you can arrange for it. The fact that the potential tenant called shows their interest in the type of property that you have. You can now start a potential tenant list. On the list, you can put the types of properties the tenants seek, so that when you see another property that matches those requirements you now have a database of people to narrow your search for a tenant.

In your rental ad, have all the necessary information:

- size of the rental,
- # bedrooms,
- # bathrooms,
- approximate location (if conditions have not been lifted yet, DO NOT include the address of the property or photos – add the address and photos to the ad after lifting conditions),
- are pets allowed,
- are utilities included,
- appliances included,
- parking,
- close by amenities,
- brief description of the rental.

Be creative with your descriptions and how you give information on price and pets. Never assume what people think, test the ad.

The following is a sample of a rental ad (for easier viewing, go to www.makemoreworklessbook.com/cashflow):

$1350 PER/Month

✉ **EMAIL THE LANDLORD**

PHONE:

📍 LARGE MAP

Address:
City:

RENTED

✉ EMAIL A FRIEND ♥ 🖨 🚩

◄◄ ▶ ▶▶   LARGER VIEW

CITY		SQUARE FOOTAGE	1080
PROPERTY TYPE	Main Floor	YEAR BUILT	1980
MONTHLY RENT	$1350.00 💬	PARKING	garage - double
SECURITY DEPOSIT	One month's rent	UNDER 18	Allowed
BEDROOMS	4	FURNISHING	Unfurnished
BATHROOMS	1	PETS	Negotiable
		DOGS	Not Allowed
		CATS	Not Allowed
		SMOKING	Non-Smoking
		AVAILABILITY DATE	Call for Availability

DESCRIPTION

Prime rental location available for the lucky renter. Lo____ bedrooms main floor suite located in Oversized double detached garage is included ____ RENTED ____nud Drive and Anthony Henday are easily accessible and the house is walking distance to sch____ ____cery stores, and especially the ravines. Public transportation is just down the road. The____ $100 monthly discount available.

Figure: 10-1 – Sample Rental Posting (courtesy of Rentfaster.ca)

Rental Price

There are a couple of ways to show your rental price. For instance, we have a few different ads for each rental property. Some will have the price listed, some will have our wanted price, and some will have a price that is $100 - $200 more than what we actually expect. Having no price on the ad may increase the amount of people who call you. They would want to call to find out what the price point is. At the very least, you got people calling and leaving you their contact information. This also shows that there is interest on the property as long as the price is right.

Having your actual price on the ad is just that – that's the price no ifs ands or buts. It also is the same as what everyone else does. So to generate more calls, you need to be different than the other ads.

Finally having higher prices can:

1. Test if you can indeed get interest at those prices and
2. Allow you to work with the tenant to give them a discount.

Have on these ads:

"$100 Discount may apply to your rent if qualified"

This will generate more calls because people always will be interested if there is potential for a discount. Think of ways you can provide a $100 or $200 discount to your tenants. For instance: on-time payment, referrals, longer-term lease, etc. These are usually things that tenants can easily accomplish. It will make them happy to be getting a discount plus you may actually get higher rents or have more security. You will have tenants who will be responsible tenants.

If you are asked about where the property is and you don't have the ability to show them the property, you can give them the address over the phone or e-mail and let them take a look around the area and the exterior beforehand. You also may at this time send them some photos that you have taken of the property. Until you lift conditions do not post photos or have the address disclosed online. The seller agent will be able to see these listings and that may cause conflict between you and the seller.

Pets

When it comes to pets, we recommend that you have on the ad "pets are negotiable." If you have the potential to increase your client base, why wouldn't you? On top of that, you are setting yourself to be a rare commodity in the rental market for those tenants who have pets. Since not many people allow pets in their rentals, you now are able to charge a monthly pet fee and/or a pet application fee. With pets, we generally charge an additional monthly fee of $30-$50 per pet. This is yet another area where you can gain points with the tenants by offering discounts.

Tip: if you are willing to rent to tenants with pets, make sure that your property is somewhat pet friendly.

Properties with very little carpeting and fenced yards are best for pets.

Parking

With regards to parking, it really depends on whether you have a detached garage with or without two separate doors or an attached garage. If you have an attached garage, generally usage of the garage is included in rent. However, if you have a detached garage, you have the opportunity to charge another $75-$150 per month for parking. Even if you weren't going to charge them, you could tell them that you have discounted the rental of the garage. If there is only one parking space, then the space will usually go to the main floor tenant. If there are two separate garage units then you will have one for each floor. Similar to the pet situation, you now have another opportunity to make your tenants feel special or maximize your cashflow.

Utilities

Utilities will generally be paid by the tenants in a rental situation. Due to the fact that the main floor will usually be a larger unit with more people living there, we usually split the utilities at 60/40 with 60 percent paid by the main floor tenant and 40 percent by the basement. This can be adjusted if the amount of people changes. For instance, if the main floor has two people and the basement has one then a 60/40 split is good. If there is three upstairs and one down a 70/30 split will be more reasonable. You can have them pay you a set lump sum based on the average utilities that you researched for a house similar to your property, have them pay as you get charged or have the tenants set utilities themselves. Generally, we prefer having a set monthly payment and reassess the amount every six months to a year, so that we can determine if the tenants are paying too much or too little for utilities. If it is too much, then it gets carried over. If not, the utilities will go up the next six months or the next term. Having the utilities on your name instead of letting the tenants set it up themselves will reduce potential conflict between your main and basement tenants, it will prevent money issues between them. Generally as the landlord you only need to provide the following: water, gas, sewage and electricity. Items such as cable, internet and phone can be set up by the tenants, since tenants may have different preferences to providers.

Summary Sheet for Investors and Money Partners

Now that you have your ads set up, taking calls and while your mortgage broker is finding you a lender, the next step is to put together a summary package of your property. This is only if you intend to have a joint venture partner or already have a joint venture partner in place. The purpose of this summary is to have all your estimated numbers, cashflow and potential split returns so that your potential joint venture partner will know what to expect for this investment opportunity. The following is what we have on our opportunity packages that we present to our potential investors:

- Photo of the property
- The details of the property: area, style, number of bedrooms, number of bathrooms, size
- Contact information
- Purchase details: Purchase price, fair market value, down payment, legal cost, renovations, inspections, appraisal, cleaning, mortgage
- Rent: main floor, basement
- Monthly expenses: mortgage, tax, insurance, miscellaneous
- Monthly cashflow
- Annual cashflow
- Forecast appreciation and equity over the next five years
- What is your role in the opportunity
- What is the role you are looking for – Joint Venture partner at 50/50 split or other
- Monthly estimated cashflow to investor
- Forecast the investment over five years and respective potential selling of the property
- Return on investment
- Option to be a money lender instead at a certain percentage rate
- Disclaimer

The following pages are a sample of our opportunity package (for easier viewing, go to www.makemoreworklessbook.com/cashflow).

Balwin Investment Opportunity

	Balwin	
Neighbourhood	Balwin	
House style	Bungalow	
	Main	Basement
# Beds	2	1
# Baths	1	1
Sq. footage	861.12	

Contact

Fong Chua	780-707-3197	fong.chua@yourarea.ca
Jessica Ng	780-709-6540	jessica.ng@yourarea.ca

Disclaimer: Rents, Mortgage cost, and Prices are subject to change and this is to be used as a guide only. All information is estimated only and buyers must perform their own due diligence to satisfaction. Appreciation rates shown are sample only and not indictive of what the Real Estate market will do but a sample projection only.

Figure: 10-2 – Sample Opportunity Package Page 1 (courtesy of AREA)

ASSURANCE REAL ESTATE ACQUISITIONS

Purchase Price		$	238,500.00
	FMV	$	245,000.00
Down Payment		$	47,700.00
Legal		$	2,000.00
Renovations		$	5,000.00
Inspections		$	498.75
Appraisal		$	225.00
Cleaning		$	200.00

Total Cash to Close	**$**	**55,623.75**

Mortgage	$	190,800.00

Monthly Income Sources

Main Level Rent	$	1,000.00
Basement Level Rent	$	800.00
Total Income	**$**	**1,800.00**

Monthly Expenses

Mortgage Payment (P&I) @ 3.5% for 30yr	$	840.88
Property Tax	$	133.33
Home Insurance (approx)	$	41.67
Miscellaneous (5% vacancy rate & 5% repairs/maintenance of Gross Rent)	$	180.00
Total Fixed Expenses	**$**	**1,195.88**

Net Monthly Cashflow	**$**	**604.12**
Net annual Cashflow	$	7,249.42

Potential future value based on the following appreciation rates:

Year	2% Appreciation	3% Appreciation	Mortgage Balance End of year	Equity @2%
2013	$ 249,900.00	$ 252,350.00	$ 187,043.90	$ 62,856.10
2014	$ 254,898.00	$ 259,920.50	$ 183,160.02	$ 71,737.98
2015	$ 259,995.96	$ 267,718.12	$ 179,144.01	$ 80,851.95
2016	$ 265,195.88	$ 275,749.66	$ 175,693.17	$ 89,502.71
2017	$ 270,499.80	$ 284,022.15	$ 170,697.49	$ 99,802.31

Disclaimer: Rents, Mortgage cost, and Prices are subject to change and this is to be used as a guide only. All information is estimated only and buyers must perform their own due diligence to satisfaction. Appreciation rates shown are sample only and not indictive of what the Real Estate market will do but a sample projection only.

Figure: 10-3 – Sample Opportunity Package Page 2 (courtesy of AREA)

ASSURANCE REAL ESTATE ACQUISITIONS

How We Can Work Together:

Parties	Contribution	Amount
You	Down payment and Renos	$ 52,700.00
AREA	Qualify for Mortgage	$ 190,800.00
	Closing costs	$ 3,002.50
	All Management work	

Scenario #1 = Joint Venture Money Partner
- 50/50 partnership
- Monthly Cashflow will be split 40% to each party and the remaining 20% will be kept in the property for miscellaneous expenses
- After each year we will all reassess to decide on selling the property or keeping the property and maintain the cashflow

ex. Net Monthly Cashflow $ 604.12
(Note: 10% contingency is factored)

Party	Cashflow per month	Annual Cashflow	Annual ROI
You (40%)	$ 241.65	$ 2,899.77	5.5%
Property (20%)	$ 120.82	$ 1,449.88	1.4%

Sell at Year		equity at 2%	Selling costs	Initial Investment	Your 50% Profit at close
1	2013	$ 62,856.10	$ 11,497.00	$ 52,700.00	$ (670.45)
2	2014	$ 71,737.98	$ 11,646.94	$ 52,700.00	$ 3,695.52
3	2015	$ 80,851.95	$ 11,799.88	$ 52,700.00	$ 8,176.03
4	2016	$ 89,502.71	$ 11,955.88	$ 52,700.00	$ 12,423.41
5	2017	$ 99,802.31	$ 12,114.99	$ 52,700.00	$ 17,493.66

Sell at Year		Your Annual Revenue	50% of Reserve	Your 50% Profit from Cashflow	Total profit to you
1	2013	$ 2,899.77	$ 724.94	$ 3,624.71	$ 2,954.26
2	2014	$ 5,799.54	$ 1,449.88	$ 7,249.42	$ 10,944.94
3	2015	$ 8,699.31	$ 2,174.83	$ 10,874.13	$ 19,050.17
4	2016	$ 11,599.08	$ 2,899.77	$ 14,498.85	$ 26,922.26
5	2017	$ 14,498.85	$ 3,624.71	$ 18,123.56	$ 35,617.21

Return on your investment if property is sold

Year	1	2	3	4	5	Cashflow ROI/yr
avg Annual ROI (@ 2% appre.)	6%	10.4%	12.0%	12.8%	14%	6.9%
avg Annual ROI (@ 3% appre.)	8%	12.8%	14.5%	15.3%	16%	

Disclaimer: Rents, Mortgage cost, and Prices are subject to change and this is to be used as a guide only. All information is estimated only and buyers must perform their own due diligence to satisfaction. Appreciation rates shown are sample only and not indictive of what the Real Estate market will do but a sample projection only.

Figure: 10-4 – Sample Opportunity Package Page 3 (courtesy of AREA)

ASSURANCE REAL ESTATE ACQUISITIONS

How We Can Work Together:

Parties	Contribution	Amount
You	Funds	$ 52,700.00
AREA	Qualify for Mortgage	$ 190,800.00
	Closing costs	$ 3,002.50
	All Management work	

Scenario #2 = Money Lender

- 8 points of return on your investment for one year

- After one year we can all reassess to extend the loan term
      or you have the option to become equity partner

- If and when the property is sold you will get your initial investment back

Total loan	$	52,700.00
Monthly Cashflow to you @ 8 points	$	351.33
Annual Cashflow	$	4,216.00

Disclaimer: Rents, Mortgage cost, and Prices are subject to change and this is to be used as a guide only. All information is estimated only and buyers must perform their own due diligence to satisfaction. Appreciation rates shown are sample only and not indictive of what the Real Estate market will do but a sample projection only.

Figure: 10-5 – Sample Opportunity Package Page 4 (courtesy of AREA)

Remember to keep the package clean and easy to follow. The package should be self-explanatory and all assumptions, if any, should be explained. Always be conservative in these numbers so that when the actual figures come, you are paying out more return than promised at first.

"Under Promise and Over Deliver"

Under promise and over deliver is a great strategy to impress and retain your investors, who will in the long run refer other potential investors to you. Just a few other comments on the package: For a joint venture, we generally like having a 50/50 split. The monthly cashflow split 50/50 and the end profits (when the property is sold, if sold) is split after all initial capital is paid back. It also is good practice to keep 20 percent of the cashflow in the property to account for miscellaneous expenses needed to maintain the property, otherwise known as contingency money. Therefore, the actually split of the cashflow is 40/40/20. If the contingency money is not utilized, then the amount is split 50/50 at the end when the property is sold. The 20 percent can be ignored if it is agreed between the parties that a set amount is kept in the property from the beginning. Generally, $5,000 to $10,000 is adequate for this contingency. You can have it set up so that when the 20 percent accumulated cashflow reaches $5,000, then the 20 percent will not be needed. Please note that in the Return On Investment of the cashflow, the final ROI of the profit and the ROI on the money lender scenario, that all opportunities result with returns higher than the returns of a traditional government savings product. This way, investors are able to compare numbers with numbers and determine where their money would be better invested. As long as your package is simple, conservative and have payouts that are higher than those of a bank then investors will be interested in your projects. To comply with regulation, never promise a specific number of percentage of return.

Due to the fact that the opportunity is an investment and one can never tell what the future holds 100 percent of the time, there always are some risks. Therefore, make sure that your tracks are covered and you have mitigated all your risks. Are your numbers conservative? Rents assumed lower than expected? Expenses assumed higher than expected? Can you sustain vacancy for three months? Six months? Did you assume higher renovation costs? Did you assume lower appreciation rates? And so forth. Three key questions to ask yourself before doing anything are:

1) What is the worst that can happen?
2) What is most likely to happen?
3) If the worst happens, can I handle it and how?

If you have truthfully answered these three questions then you have assessed the risk of what you are doing or getting into. To protect yourself further, a disclaimer is very important to have on your opportunity package that you present to your investors or partners. The following is what you can use:

Disclaimer: Rents, mortgage cost, and prices are subject to change and this is to be used as a guide only. All information is estimated and investors must perform their own due diligence to satisfaction. Appreciation rates shown are sample and not indicative of what the real estate market will do.

By having the necessary precautions in place and assessing your numbers conservatively, you will have managed your risks adequately and allow you to Make More and Work less with Cashflow and with peace of mind.

Less is more, be clear and accurate with what you want your audience to know.

<u>Chapter 10 - Due Diligence Part II:</u>
<u>Rental Market</u>

Take advantage of every opportunity to practice your communication skills so that when important occasions arise, you will have the gift, the style, the sharpness, the clarity, and the emotions to affect other people.

- Jim Rohn -

Assurance Keys to Your Success

- Post rental ad for maximum exposure

- Be different – find ways to give your tenants discounts

- Create summary sheet for investors

- Under promise, over deliver

- Clean, simple and easy

- SECTION 3 -

Relationships and Maintenance

In the end, it all comes full circle. Relationships, relationships and relationships is key to any venture, property, deal and opportunity. Without relationships, nothing will get done well. As long as we focus on creating WOW experiences by adding value to the relationships that we build, then, it will come back to us in record amounts. These are the relationships that will essentially get you to Make More and Work Less with Cashflow while everyone else also benefits.

213

Chapter - 11 -

Finding Investors: Communicating and Connecting Are Keys

It only takes one person, one deal and one opportunity to change your world.

- JT Foxx -

The other day we decided to catch up with John and Melissa and see how they were doing. Having just closed on a property, we were curious how they were handling the great news. John picked up and answered, "Everything is great! We are very excited and ready to get things moving. Unfortunately, we haven't had a lot of luck finding investors to help with the financial side of things. Any thoughts?"

215

MAKE MORE WORK LESS with CASHFLOW

Relational Capital

Now that you know how to find the property, the next question that usually comes up is, "How do I finance it?" After all, we only have a finite amount of money. Once we run out of our own money, we can't do any more deals without the help of investors. The key to finding investors to partner with you on deals is what Nido Qubein calls "Relational Capital." What does relational capital mean? It is much like financial capital. Instead of having access to a lot of monetary capital, you are rich in relationships. That is, you have a deep and solid connection with many people who believe in you and will help you financially.

Communication

Since relational capital is the key, it is only natural to ask ourselves, "How do we build relational capital?" This all ties back to Chapter 3, where we learned how to focus first on providing value to others and to avoid the car salesman stereotype. As long as you keep focusing on providing value to others, you will continue to attract people to you. For investors, there are some extra steps you will need to take to ensure that he or she will continue to want to work with you. The key - is the word "Communication."

We have found that many investors understand the risks of investing. Whether it is the stock market, mutual funds, exempt markets or real estate, an investor understands that there could be little gains, big gains, no gains or losses. What makes them trust someone is the level of communication they get from the person who has their money.

To illustrate this, let's think about an example:

Bob is a wealthy man and had invested a significant portion of his savings to real estate property ABC. He was told that it was a 12-unit building and that it would cashflow about $800 for his portion in the property. A year down the road, his buddies who had laughed at him for investing in real estate property ABC, sent him an article they had found indicating that the property is facing some financial trouble. Once Bob saw this, he called the representative that had sold him the investment. No response. He called and e-mailed repeatedly asking for information and still no response. He also noticed that he no longer received any of his allocated cashflow for the past three months. Finally, in anger, he took measures to find out what his options are from a lawyer. He is now thinking about suing or even foreclosing on the property.

Now let's think of an alternative way of handling that situation:

Bob is a wealthy man and had invested a significant portion of his savings to real estate property ABC. He was told that it was a 12-unit building and that it would cashflow about $800 for his portion in the property. A year down the road, his buddies who had laughed at him for investing in real estate property ABC, sent him an article they had found indicating that the property is facing some financial trouble. Once Bob saw this, he

218

called the representative that had sold him the investment. No response. Two hours later, the representative called Bob back. He apologized to Bob that he had to hear about this from his friends and went on to explain to Bob that one of the other investors that had been part of the deal had defaulted on their responsibilities and pulled out of the deal. This left them without 30 percent of the original investment. The representative explained that they are working late with the entire team to find a new investor to fill this hole and told Bob that his cashflow will be taking a hit until they can find a new investor as the cashflow will be used to cover any deficiency with the missing investment. Once Bob heard about this, he understood the problems the company had and went on to find out if he was able to invest more of his available capital in the deal.

Although this is a fictional story, you can see that Bob reacted differently based on the information he received. The level of communication was different. When you try to hide things from your investors, thinking that you are "protecting" them from worry, you could actually be causing more trouble in the future if they hear about it from another source.

Communication is Not Enough, Connect with your Investor

Do you ever wonder why when you ask a friend to bring you your books and they end up asking you "*you want me to buy hooks?*" or question why a person would ask you at a drive through if you want to pay an extra 25 cents for unlimited refills? How about this next one? We walk by someone and he or she says *"Hi, how are you doing?"* and before you can answer he or she says *"Great!"* and walks away. What is happening to our society now is that yes, we are communicating, we talk, we hear, we see and we scribble, but what we are not doing is connecting. We need to speak, not just talk, listen not just hear, observe not merely see and write not just scribble.

Communication Versus Connection

Nido Qubein, one of the top businessmen in the world shared his thoughts about the difference between connecting and communicating. It all stems from our society focusing too much on training instead of educating. Our education system now is training the younger generation to become business people, engineers, doctors and lawyers. Our work places are putting employees into training programs and training cashiers and sales clerks for customer service. What businesses and our education systems are not doing enough of is educating. When we train, we show you the HOW. When we educate, we show you the WHY. Training is transactional and technical, whereas education is transformational and stays with you forever when the training is long forgotten. Nido stresses that he is not saying that training is not needed. Training is provided if you want someone to do what you want them to do, but training alone cannot stand. Just as communicating and selling alone are not enough without connecting and positioning. By educating, we learn how to BE while with training, we learn what to do. In school, we are trained how to count. From our parents, we are taught *what* counts. We must learn to speak and listen, observe and write. By doing so, we will connect and when we connect, something happens – heart-to-heart, soul-to-soul, mission-to-mission with another human being.

As with each deal, each investor is different. It is up to you to figure out what level of communication and connection each investor wants. Some want the nitty, gritty details, down to the last number while others only want a high level summary of what is happening. This will change the way you present things to your investor. Some will take action based on emotion and feel. In that case, you would like to work with the experience of the investment, the feel of working together and the emotional freedom being away from other traditional investments. What must you BE so that your investor can connect with you? How must your potential investor FEEL so that they will invest in you?

Investors want security. All investors will want to know what security they have so that you won't run off with their money. It is in your best interest to ensure that they are satisfied with the level of protection you are giving them. There are many things you can do to help them feel comfortable that their investment is secured with you. You could have their name on title so that they will retain ownership of the house; you could have the joint venture agreement written in a way that protects their interest and register it against the property or other ways suggested by your lawyer. Once an investor knows that their investment is secured and they will be protected, their objections will decrease.

221

Warm Versus Cold Market

Now that we know how to retain investors, we can move onto how to find them. There are two types of markets available to you in the world. A warm market and a cold market. A warm market includes all the people that you have interacted with before, such as your family and friends. They know of you already and know your character. A cold market is anyone who is a stranger. You will modify your approach based on the type of person and market.

For a warm market, you already have built the relationship, and you may be able to go straight to the topic of investing with you, if you believe you are close enough to talk about it. If not, you will need to spend some time to enhance the relationship using tips in Chapter 3 before you talk about' investing. For some people in your warm market, they may not want to invest with you, or may not be able to, but you can always ask them if they know of someone who may be interested. This is called referral marketing – *ask for an introduction.* Remember, everyone is separated by six degrees. With the Internet and social media, many say that it is as little as three degrees now. It only takes one person, one deal and one opportunity to change your world.

For a cold market, you will have to go the long route of building the relationship first. For people in a cold market, you will find them either through referral marketing or by posting your deal online, either on your Web site or any other Web sites available to you.

Regardless of the market, the most effective tool available to you is the use of a summary sheet. A summary sheet can be as detailed or as simple as you want it to be. The level of details likely will depend on which type of investor you are targeting. As we have mentioned before, some people want the nitty, gritty details while others want just the simple summary. Our suggestion would be to prepare both sheets and start off with the simple one. As you are presenting the deal to your investor, you will be able to gauge whether he or she wants more details or not. You can even let them know that you have a more detailed sheet if they would like to take a look at it. Please refer back to Chapter 10 for details of a summary sheet.

Handling Objections

The most effective way we have found to handle any objections that an investor could have with the return on investment is to compare the returns they can expect to get with your opportunity to what they can expect to get with their traditional means of investing. More often than not, once you educate them and show them that they will be making more with you in a more secured way, they will begin to understand that they no longer have a reason to say no.

Return on investment is not the only concern of the investors. Questions such as:

What if the housing market goes down?
What if the tenants run off?
What if the tenants damage the property?
What if I need my money back for an emergency?

What if we can't find a buyer in the future?
What if you run off on me?

The best way to deal with these situations is to mention them before the investor does. After you bring up these concerns, make sure you provide a solution to each. In many cases, the investor may not have even thought of the concerns that you mention. Since you have brought up the issues yourself and also provide a solution to them, your potential investor will be a lot more comfortable to be investing with you, as you have shown that you have their best interest in mind. Make sure that you have done your research and know what the risks are, so that you are able to provide the necessary solutions to all potential risks because there are those who will come up with concern after concern. There will come a time where you will realize that some people are not the best fit for a partnership. As the Henry Ford saying goes "*Whether you think you can or you think you can't, you are right.*" Some people will go and find reasons that the opportunity will not work regardless of any risk management that you have provided. Make sure that you have outlined what the risks are, what you have done to assure that the risks are managed and what your exit strategies are so that your investor can make their best assessment on your opportunity.

Another really effective way to deal with objections is to acknowledge the objection and then ask a question. Sometimes, the investor's concern is not really what the objection is, but it is a deeper concern. When someone says that "*the investment is too expensive*" sometimes what they really mean is they do not see the value of the investment. Hence, it is your job to ask the right questions to find out what really concerns them. Before you ask the question, always acknowledge their concern first and then ask.

For example:

> *Potential Investor: "Why should I invest with you if I can go elsewhere that is better?"*
>
> *You: "I understand your concerns as it is a lot of money that we are dealing with here. I too would be considering many options before I settle on one. What, if you do not mind me asking, are the other opportunities that you are looking at offering you?*
>
> *Potential Investor: "They are looking for less money in and are giving a larger return!"*
>
> *You: "Wow! I would be considering them too if I were you. What exactly are they offering? What is your security?"*
>
> *Potential Investor: "Well, I don't have any security on the property but my return is $50 higher than what you are offering each month!"*
>
> *You: "I see, thank you for mentioning that. Wouldn't you say that $50 would be a good peace of mind knowing that I wouldn't run off on you leaving you with nothing? Wouldn't you like to tell your friends that you have the title under your name so that if anything happens you have a say as to what is done to the property?"*

See how the conversation is an actual discussion, instead of constant debating on statistics? It opens the conversation up to creative solutions and an opportunity to build a relationship. It allows for both you and the investor to get to know each other and become partners on the opportunity being discussed.

As long as you are honest, conservative with your numbers, adding value to your partners and ensure that you are communicating and connecting with them at their level of need and want, you always will find and retain the right people that will assist you to Make More and Work Less with Cashflow.

The more value you provide,
the stronger relationships become.

Chapter 11 – Finding Investors: Communicating and Connecting Are Keys

How must one FEEL for them to do what you would like them to do?

- Nido Qubein -

Assurance Keys to Your Success

- Build relational capital - deep and solid connection to others

- Communication and Connections are keys

- Who must you BE to work with your investor

- How must your investor FEEL?

- Provide security for your investor

- Warm versus cold markets

- Bring up concerns before your investor can

- Provide solutions to all risks possible

- Manage risks and provide exit strategies

- Acknowledge and ask questions when objected

- Be honest, conservative and ALWAYS add value

Chapter - 12 -

Finding Tenants:
Caring Is Key

**A relationship is more than finding the right person.
It's also about being the right person.**

- Unknown -

John and Melissa called one day, "Using the method you told us, we were able to find an investor to partner with us on our latest property! We can't tell you how exciting that is. What about finding tenants? How are we supposed to advertise for them? How do we set up the viewings? Where do we start? What do we tell them if they are interested?"

Many times, you hear horror stories about bad tenants and what they did. That's why it is so important to carefully screen your tenants and make sure you put in the right tenant, rather than just any tenant. Sometimes, you will want to put in a tenant right away to start making money, but in the long run, it always will pay to wait for a good tenant. It will end up costing you less. Great tenants are an important factor to Make More and Work Less with Cashflow.

Tenant Search

Now how do we find tenants? We will first need to advertise for them. We can't merely wait around and hope someone will notice an empty house that needs to be rented. There are a few places where you can post an ad, including the Internet and paper. By putting ads up in both media, you will ensure that you get both the people who search the Internet and the people who search the papers.

We have found that a good place to advertise online is kijiji.com. There are many other places as well that will show up through a Google search. These are also good sources in determining how much to set the rent. Just like looking at the comparables, you will want to find properties that are similar to yours to determine the rent amount you should charge.

In your ad, you will want to put yourself in the other person's shoes. How must that person feel about the ad to want to give you a call? This is similar to the previous chapter about connecting rather than communicating. Sometimes you will find that it takes about two weeks for more people to start noticing your ad. However, if you have waited for over a month already, chances are great, you have priced the rent too high and you will need to lower the price. There is no right or wrong way to price your property. It is just a matter of what the market is ready to accept.

In your ad, you may choose to put up the rental price or not. This will be an area you need to test to see what works best for you. You may even choose to have a price up in one ad and no price in another ad. If you choose to put up the rental price, then you will ensure that the people who call you are likely able to afford the price. However, you may have found that you have misjudged the rental amount that you can charge and underpriced it. Now, you will have to honor the rental amount you advertised if you find a great tenant. On the other hand, if you don't put up the price, you will likely get calls from many people, including people that may not be able to afford the rental amount you have in mind. The good thing about this method is that you can adjust the pricing you tell people based on the number of responses you receive.

Word-of-mouth is another great method of spreading the word. Although it may be old-fashioned, you never know how effective it could be until you try it. Ask your current tenants for new ones. Chances are great that family and friends they recommend will have similar traits and personalities as your tenants. Since you have approved your tenants already, there is a good chance that their referrals are potentially good tenants as well. If you do not have tenants, then make sure you ask other investors and landlords. You will be surprised how many potentially good tenants are turned away because investors/landlords do not have the rental situation at the moment that is a right fit for the tenant. You may very well be that person who does have the right fit! Ask people at nearby apartments and condos, family and friends, the more people you tell the faster you will find a quality tenant.

Taking the Call

Once you have your ad up and have told everyone you know, you soon will start getting calls or emails. When that happens, remember it is good news for you! It is easy to panic and wonder if you know how to do this the first few times, but once you get the hang of it, you will adjust and excel. A good strategy is to allow the calls to go to your voice mail, this will allow you to get your information and questions together and be ready to talk to a potential tenant instead of being caught off guard answering the phone as soon as it rings. Once you are ready and have an allotted time to call, return the call and have a conversation with the potential tenant. Now what do we say to potential tenants?

If you do choose to pick up the phone right away, the first thing you want to do is thank them for their interest in your rental. Then remember to ask them for their full name, e-mail and phone number. You can let them know the reason you are asking for their number is in case you get disconnected. That way, you will have a way to reach them if you need to do so, rather than hoping that they will call again. Especially, if they tell you that they will think about it, or talk to someone about it first. Now, you have their number to see if they are still interested at a later time. Remember to also ask which way they would prefer to be contacted. Whether it is by text messaging, e-mail, home phone or cell phone, make sure that you have all contact information. The last thing you want is to send them an e-mail and find out later that they only check e-mails once a week. You will be surprised how many people actually prefer text messaging as it is easy and instant for those who may not be able to take a phone call at work or other situations. Responding by email also allows you to get your information and questions together, which will save you time and effort.

From there, you can ask them what it is they would like to know about the property. You may find it helpful to prepare yourself a summary sheet so you can read off it instead of telling them information from your memory. We would suggest that you keep to the basic information such as how many bedrooms, bathrooms, and rent amount. If you give too much information, people would feel overwhelmed and will likely feel too confused to take action.

Make sure you listen and let them do the talking. When they ask a question, then you can answer. As every person will ask different questions, we can only give guidelines of what you can do. We suggest you also ask questions yourself. We have prepared some questions below, along with why you should ask questions along these lines.

How many people are planning on being in the property?

This will let you know how many people to expect. If you have a one bedroom rental, and three people are planning on moving in, you should question why they are looking for such a small place for three people.

Will there be any pets?

If you have decided that you don't want any pets in your properties, this will eliminate them right away. If you do allow pets, you will know that you can charge a little extra depending on what type of pet it is. We normally do not charge for fish as they cannot damage the property by being there while it is easier to charge for cats and dogs that could be harder on the property.

How did you hear about us?

This will allow you to track your marketing. Is your ad in one place working better than in another place? If you never get calls from a certain ad, you could focus more of your resources on the ads that is getting you replies, rather than on the ads that doesn't get you replies. If they were referred to you by someone else, it is a great opportunity for you to show your appreciation to that person and send them a gift or a sincere "Thank You" card. This will encourage more referrals from them.

Why are you looking for a place?

This will provide you with some insight as to why the person calling is looking for a place. Perhaps their previous landlord is selling the place and they need a new place to live, or maybe they are being evicted, or they could be looking to move out of their parent's home. By asking this question, you can more easily gauge the motivation of your potential tenant.

What do you do and how long have you done this?

This will allow you to gauge whether or not the potential tenant can afford renting the place from you. The last thing you want to do is put a tenant in who may need to choose between eating and paying the rent. Depending on the company, you will be able to see if they are credible and whether you will be able to check references. How long that person has worked there also will show job security and job loyalty. These are all traits that you would like in a future tenant.

There are many more questions that you can ask, but just keep in mind that this isn't an interrogation session. Your intent is to get them to want to view your property while quickly gauging them to ensure they won't waste your time. When you meet them in person at your property, you can then ask more questions.

Before you end the call, make sure you ask them if they have any other questions you can answer for them. You also will want to make an appointment with your potential tenant for a viewing at the property. If you have been getting many calls, you should plan to make the viewings every 30-45 minutes apart. By making the viewings every 30-45 minutes apart, you will accomplish three things.

1) It will show the people coming that there are other people interested
2) If someone doesn't show, you aren't waiting for a long time and
3) Maximizes your time so that you will not need to go back and forth showing the property multiple times.

Yes, unfortunately, sometimes people just don't show up. Instead of taking this personally, keep in mind that if they didn't have the intent to show up, then chances are great that you wouldn't have wanted them as tenants anyway. So, look forward to the ones that do show and focus your attention on them. They are potentially good tenants.

Follow up and Application Form

Right after the call, make sure that you send the potential tenant a follow up e-mail. In this e-mail, you will summarize everything that was discussed and details about the property. Again: number of bedrooms, number of bathrooms, how utilities are handled, laundry situation, pet fees, size of unit, location and any specific items that were discussed during your phone conversation. Also included in this e-mail are the rental application form and what the initial deposit is if they are interested. Ask them to fill out the form in its entirety.

This is one of many screening methods that you have. Tell them that for you to do what is needed to get them into the unit smoothly, that you will need them to fill in the information asked and to bring it to the showing or send it to you in advance. You will find that those who do not fill out the application already are someone you do not want to be renting to. It shows that they are not good at following directions or that they are not interested enough to do the necessary steps to get the unit. If someone chooses to fill out the form, but not send it to you until they look at the property and see if they are interested, that is OK too, as it shows that they are still willing to do work upfront. Also, in the application form is the request of a possible credit check. You will find that this will help weed out those who know they are not going to get the unit due to poor credit and will not fill out the application or become disinterested in the unit. It also will help you determine the character of certain potential tenants who know they have bad credit but will come out and tell you honestly that they have bad credit, why and what they are doing to fix it.

WARNING: You will be getting a lot of sob stories and it is really up to you whether you trust their story or not. Be objective and strong.

This is where the rest of the information is needed. Along with the credit check request is their current and past jobs and supervisors, current and past landlords' names and contact information. You will see an example of the application form on the later pages.

The initial deposit amount does not need to be a large sum, but we suggest that it be significant enough (a few hundred dollars in most markets) to ensure that the potential tenants are serious about the property, $200 to $500.

At times, you will find that the potential tenants will ask if they can send the application to you earlier. In these cases, you can suggest fax, which is secured. However, if you do not have a fax machine, you can suggest e-mail. A note of caution on this though; e-mail is not a secured medium to send private information through, and with some sensitive information requested on the application, you will need to advise them that it isn't secured and that they are sending it at their own risk. Our personal preference is to receive it at the showing as this will allow you to look at it and ask them questions in person. However, most applicants are willing to send in a partially filled out application form (with only their security identification numbers missing), which they will then fill out after seeing the unit. This is also preferred only if the applicant requests it. This allows you to check employment and rental history before you meet the applicant which can save you time as well.

The day before and of the viewing, give your potential tenants a call or text to ensure that they are still planning on going to the viewing. If they aren't, then you can free up the spot for someone else who is interested. This will help you manage your time and will give you less frustration if people don't show. You also should remind them to bring the filled out application form (if you haven't previously received it) and the initial deposit if they are interested.

Another way that potential tenants may contact you is via e-mail. When you get the e-mails, make sure you respond within 24 hours. If you don't, chances are great the potential tenants will find you unprofessional, or think that the property already has been rented. This could cost you a potentially good tenant. In your return e-mail to them, you could follow the same guidelines.

Keeping Good Records

In both cases, make sure you keep notes on what was discussed. It is hard to remember every detail about someone you have never met, and keeping it in writing will always help you recall details about your conversation. This also will show your potential tenant that you are attentive and when you repeat details they have told you, such as children or pet names, they will feel more connected to you. You will be surprised how impressed and open the potential tenants are when you remember certain details from conversations that you have discussed with them before. This will go a long way when building a good tenant-landlord relationship allowing you to ultimately Make More and Work Less with Cashflow.

Now that you have several viewings arranged, we can move on to what to do when your potential tenants show up!

As another added bonus to you, we have included a sample application form. Use it or modify it to your liking that will enable you to Make More and Work Less with Cashflow.

Go to www.makemoreworklessbook.com/cashflow to download your template.

Application for Rental Accommodation

The Landlord Acknowledges the Confidentiality of This Document
(Must Be Fully Completed)

1. ACCOMMODATION INFORMATION: Date of Application: _____

Address of Premises: _____

Type Requested: ☐1 bedroom   ☐2 bedrooms   ☐3 bedrooms   ☐Other _____

Date Requested: Day _____   Month _____   Year _____

Names of all people to occupy the premises:

Adults _____

Children _____

2. PERSONAL INFORMATION OF APPLICANTS:

(1ˢᵗ Adult)

Full Name: _____   Birth date: _____

Present Address: _____   Phone: _____

_____   How Long: _____

Previous Address: _____

_____   How Long: _____

SIN #: _____

Drivers License: _____

(2ⁿᵈ Adult)

Full Name: _____   Birth date: _____

Present Address: _____   Phone: _____

_____   How Long: _____

Previous Address: _____

_____   How Long: _____

SIN #: _____

Drivers License: _____

3. EMPLOYMENT INFORMATION OF APPLICANTS:

(1ˢᵗ Adult)

Current Employer: _____   Occupation: _____

Supervisor: _____   How long: _____

Address: _____   Phone: _____

Previous Employer: _____   Occupation: _____

Supervisor: _____   How long: _____

Address: _____   Phone: _____

(2ⁿᵈ Adult)

Current Employer: _____   Occupation: _____

Supervisor: _____   Phone: _____

Address: _____   How long: _____

Previous Employer: _____   Occupation: _____

Figure: 12-1 – Sample Rental Application Page 1 (courtesy of AREA)

Supervisor: _____ Phone: _____
Address: _____ How long: _____

4. **CREDIT INFORMATION OF APPLICANTS:**

(1st Adult)

Income: _____ per month (net after tax)

Bank: _____ Branch: _____

Credit references:

Name: _____ Phone: _____
Name: _____ Phone: _____

(2nd Adult)

Income: _____ per month (net after tax)

Bank: _____ Branch: _____

Credit references:

Name: _____ Phone: _____
Name: _____ Phone: _____

5. **RENTAL HISTORY:**

(1st Adult)

Current Landlord: _____ Phone: _____
Previous Landlord: _____ Phone: _____

(2nd Adult)

Current Landlord: _____ Phone: _____
Previous Landlord: _____ Phone: _____

6. **ADDITIONAL INFORMATION:**

7. **RELATIVES OR FRIENDS WHO CAN BE CONTACTED IN CASE OF EMERGENCY:**

1st Adult ___ *2nd Adult*

Name: _____ Name: _____
Address: _____ Address: _____
Phone #: _____ Phone #: _____
Relationship: _____ Relationship: _____

Approval of this application is subject to the Landlord and Tenant signing a Residential Tenancy Agreement.

☐ *Additional Details of Applicant Provided on a Separate Attached Sheet*

All statements that I have made in this application are true. I authorize the Landlord to do a credit check and criminal background check. By signing this application, **ALL** personal information **is consensually given** for use by us or our appointed agents in respect to your application, subsequent tenancy, or on- file records in accordance to The Personal Information Protection and Electronic Documents Act (PIPEDA 2004) This is to include and extend to the gathering and consent to access of account information and status for ALL utility companies that the Tenant may enter into contracts with for the duration and for periods after the termination of the tenancy to ensure accounts are in good and current standing during and at the completion of the lease period.

_____ Dated this _____ day of _____, ____.
Signature of 1st Applicant

_____ Dated this _____ day of _____, ____.
Signature of 2nd Applicant

_____ Dated this _____ day of _____, 20____.
Signature of 3rd Applicant

Figure: 12-2 – Sample Rental Application Page 2 (courtesy of AREA)

WOW EXPERIENCES

*The more you envision yourself from
the other person's perspective,
the better the experience you are able to provide.*

Chapter 12 – Finding Tenants: Caring Is Key

Every good relationship is based on respect. If it's not based on respect, nothing that appears to be good will last very long.

- Amy Grant -

Assurance Keys to Your Success

- Wait for a good tenant - it will cost less long term

- The more people you tell the faster you find a tenant

- Use multiple ads and track what is most effective

- Ask for all methods of contact

- Do not bombard them with questions

- Schedule viewings 30-45 minutes apart

- Send follow up e-mail along with application form

- Ask questions you know the answers to

- Confirm with applicant before viewing

- Keep good records and refer to details of past conversations

Chapter - 13 -

Showings and Screenings: Their Best Intentions

There is a saying every nice piece of work needs the right person in the right place at the right time.

- Benoit Mandelbrot –

A couple days later Melissa sent us an e-mail: "Hey! We've been getting tons of calls on the rental. I've been taking down their information just like you suggested, but what are we suppose to do when they show up"? We chuckled and replied: "Great news! Don't worry about it, we'll show you the way."

There are three very important stages to screening potential tenants: Succeeding in these stages will allow you to Make More and Work Less with Cashflow when dealing with this property.

> 1) First point of contact (phone/email) that we discussed in the previous chapter
> 2) Meeting
> 3) Background check

Once you have established the first point of contact, you will know whether the potential tenants are serious about renting or not. If they have not bothered to fill out the application, that usually means that they have something to hide or are not interested enough in your property to fill it out. Whatever the reason is, you will have saved yourself a lot of time from meeting and interviewing a potential tenant in person who is not interested.

Confirming the Meeting

As discussed in the previous chapter, prior to the viewings you have arranged, contact the potential tenants to save you some time from people not showing. While this can still happen, it will decrease the chance of someone not showing up. For those that still do not show up, don't lose heart! It means you probably wouldn't have wanted them as tenants in the first place if they already are giving you heart aches!

Look for Signs of a Great Tenant

When the potential tenants show up at the property, we suggest that you walk to their car and greet them. This will give you a chance to peek inside their car. Is it messy? If so, the odds of them keeping your property tidy may not be so high. This is not necessarily indicative of their personality, however, it is a consideration you can take into account. In extreme cases, if the car is jammed packed full of things, this could be a large warning sign for you. They could be hoarders, or they possibly don't have a place to live right now. At this point, if you feel that it is appropriate to ask, mention it. As we discussed at the beginning of the book, how people are dressed also is very important. Now, we are not saying that they need to be dressed up in a suit and tie, but are they clean cut; presentable; sloppy; etc? How they interact with you also is very important. Are they well mannered, do they seem like happy people, are they energetic or quiet? You will find that the initial gut instinct that you get when first meeting the potential tenant will go a long way with your decision-making. If you have a good feel right at the beginning, you will find more things about the potential tenant throughout the meeting that will encourage you to rent to them.

WARNING: Do not let your emotions drive your decision. Even if you have a really good feeling about someone, do not let that cloud your decision if there are a lot of red flags.

Therefore, it is highly recommended that you and your partner (or someone else) be there for the showing/meeting process. It is always good to have a second opinion on potential tenants. Your partner may have a different feel of them initially or noticed something that you didn't realize yourself. This allows you to discuss and compare notes when the time comes to make a decision.

Build Rapport! Not an Interrogation!

The more you ask, the more you will learn about the person. Now, we are not asking you to interrogate them with endless questions, but you can include it as you make conversation. Unfortunately, there is no science to how to build rapport with a person and how to tell if the potential tenant will be a good candidate for you and your property.

There are however, some tips we can provide you with on how to build rapport and some tips of what you would want to look for to help you gauge a person.

Let's first start with how to build rapport. You will realize that people love to talk about themselves. As we have mentioned before, the intent is not to interrogate a person, but to learn about a person. You should be interested in hearing what they have to say, and in some cases, you will hear a person's life story. Be patient and know that some of what they say will help you in deciding if they are good candidates or not. If they are constantly talking about what kind of trouble they've had in the past, ask yourself this: What are the chances of it happening again? To us, the chances are quite high. What makes things different this time around? While it is hard hearing someone's sad story, it is better to avoid giving yourself heart ache in the future by allowing emotion to rule your decision. In the business of real estate, emotion is what will get you in trouble. Our suggestion for you is to keep business strictly business.

If you want to do something for that person, there are many other ways to do things including volunteering your help if you so desire or recommending them to members of your team who can assist them.

Some questions you can ask that usually helps to build rapport and understanding of your potential tenant are shown here. Keep in mind that no one person is the same and they will respond to these questions differently. If you sense that they are uncomfortable with any questions, then you could move onto another branch of questions.

Note that questions could vary depending on the age of your potential tenant:

- Family.
    o Do you have family here?
    o Do you have any kids?
    o Do you have any pets?
    o Where are you from?
    o Do you have a big family?
    o Are you close to your family?

- Work.
    o Where do you work? (This would be on the application, so if you got it ahead of time, you can mention where they work and move on to the next question)
    o How are you enjoying your work?
    o What are your duties at work?
    o How long have you been working there?
    o What are you planning on doing in the future?

- Hobbies.
  - What do you like to do with your free time? (Depending on their answer, you can vary your next question)
  - Which sport/games do you like?
  - What are you good at? Or really enjoy doing?

By asking questions to build rapport, you will find that you and your potential tenants may have some things in common. This will be helpful to you as people tend to like people who like the same things as them. Find as many things that you have in common or know and discuss about them with the potential tenant. By doing so, the tenant will remember you and enjoy your company. Remember, even if you really like a potential tenant, chances are great, they have been to a lot of other rentals as well. So not only are you trying to make sure you are putting the right tenant into your property, but also they are searching for the right property and landlord. If it came down to two rentals they may very well choose your unit because both of you shared the same favorite restaurant or have common interests.

Now that you know how to connect with a person, here are some questions you can ask to help gauge what kind of tenant they will be. We suggest that you mix up the questions between building rapport and gathering information. This will make the conversation flow much smoother without seeming to interrogate them.

- Do you or anyone staying here smoke?
- Do you stay home a lot?
- Why are you looking for a place?

- What is your current living situation?
- How is your pet with others?
- What is your work schedule like?
- Do you watch your friend's pets much?

We have given you a lot of questions that you can ask your potential tenants. Chances are they will have questions for you as well. Make sure you give them an opportunity to ask the questions they have as well. Questions they will likely ask will be related to the property and tenancy (rental, utilities, what's included, etc.). At the end, prior to them leaving, just check again and ask them if they have any concerns.

At this time, we would like to point out that if you have a suited property, it also would be a good idea to ask questions regarding if they have any concerns with your other tenants. For example, if your tenants already living there have pets or kids, you can ask them if they have any problems with dogs, since your other tenants has a dog. Not only will this allow you to make a good decision, but it also shows that you care for your tenants. It shows that you have your existing tenant's best interest in mind and also theirs as you want them both to have a good living situation. This way the potential tenant will compare the questions you ask with other landlords and get a feel as to who will be concerned for them more.

If you haven't already received the application, do so now if the potential tenant is still interested. You will find that some people are reluctant to give you their private information until after they know that they are interested in the place. You can also collect the initial deposit now too. Make sure you give them a receipt and inform them that if they are selected, the money will be applied to the first month's rent and if they are not selected, then the money will be returned to them. Note that their deposit will not be returned to them if they decided to not take the unit after you have already confirmed with them that they got the unit. This is because once a deposit is taken, it means that the unit is locked. If they are putting the deposit down that means that no one else can see the property, therefore if they decided that they no longer want the property, you would have lost a lot of time where you could have showed the property. However if you have decided not to rent to the potential tenants due to whatever reason, then the deposit should be returned.

Actions to Take After Showing

Once the showing is over, make sure you write down what you remember from your conversation with them. As mentioned in the previous chapter, always keep good records. This will prompt your memory of the potential tenants when you are trying to decide who would be the best fit for you and your property.

Now that the showing is over, you can do the rest of your due diligence. This would include any reference check and credit check using the information you gathered with the application form.

Trust but Verify

It is important to call the references on the application form to confirm the stories that your potential tenant is telling you. In the end, it comes down to your gut feeling of the potential tenant. Trust your gut but do not believe everything they or their references tell you. Ask questions that will test what their stories are and whether their answers are consistent. Remember, it is not an interrogation, so you don't have you ask all the questions you can think of.

Questions to Ask the References

Former landlord:
- What was it like renting to (potential tenant name)?
- Did they have parties?
- Were they noisy?
- Did they pay rent on time?
- What was the property like after they left?
- Do you have other rental properties?
- If you had the chance would you rent to them again?
- Why did they stop renting from you?
- What was the rent they were paying?
- How long did you rent to them?
- What three characteristics would you use to describe them?

Work reference:
- How is your business doing?
- What is their work ethic?
- Do they show up to work on time?
- Do they work well with others at work?
- What was their role at work?
- Are they hard working?
- Do you have any issues with them?
- Is their job secure for the time being?
- Do you see them moving up with your company?

- What three characteristics would you use to describe them?

These questions will allow you to do a few things: determine if the reference is legitimate and actually people that were their supervisors or landlords instead of friends pretending to be their supervisors or landlords; allows you to check and see if the stories and information the potential tenant is telling you are true and consistent; and finally gauge what type of relationships your potential tenant develops. If they are good tenants, they will always have good partings with their previous landlords and great feedback from their work places. Remember to ask a few questions that you already know the answer. This will allow you to make sure the answers are consistent among all parties and between conversations.

As mentioned before, there is no science as to how to interview a potential tenant or how to check their references.

By asking questions, you can arm yourself with some information and insight into their personality and sense if there are any red flags. In the end, it will come down to your gut feel about the person.

Even with careful screening you can still expect that on average, for every 10 tenants you have, there may be two tenants that require more attention. By following your gut, going through their references, asking the right questions and being firm on what you expect of your tenants, you will minimize the risk of having bad tenants. As you become more experienced, you will have a better idea of what questions you should ask. Careful screening for great tenants will lead to great potential to Make More and Work Less with Cashflow.

Putting yourself into other people's situation will allow you to think of ways to WOW the relationship.

Chapter 13 – Showings and Screening: Their Best Intentions

The way I become friends with somebody is a slow process. You can't just spill your guts and tell them everything about yourself and expect them to listen and understand you because you don't know them."

- Leighton Meester -

Assurance Keys to Your Success

- Confirm the meeting and showing time

- First impressions – What is your initial feel for them?

- Build a relationship, build rapport. Not an interrogation

- Ask about their family, work and hobbies

- Find common interests with your potential tenant

- Ask questions about how they get along with others

- Show concern for your existing tenants

- Make sure you have a filled out application form

- Trust but verify – call references, ask questions you know the answers to

Chapter - 14 -

Managing Properties
The Easy Way

**Nobody cares how much you know
until they know how much you care.**

- Theodore Roosevelt -

A week has gone by since we last heard from John. We decided to drive by the property and see what was happening. To our surprise, we saw John and Melissa in the property cleaning up and looking after minor odds and ends. They saw us, welcomed us in and said: "Hey! We were just about to call you! We have renters coming tomorrow! Should we have something prepared for them? How do you manage your properties?"

To manage properties the easy way, there are two parts to this. The first is the possession of the property by your tenant and the second is the period of time the tenant is renting the property. If you would like to Make More and Work Less with Cashflow, these two parts must be dealt with exceptionally well.

You Get What You Give

The first thing you should know is that if you want to have great tenants you must treat your tenants great, and to do so you must start great. This is where you show your tenant that you care. After all, no one likes to be mistreated and everyone likes someone who cares for him or her. Always put yourself in your tenants shoes and just consider what would they think if you did something a certain way.

Congratulate your Tenant and give them a Clear Path!

After you have selected your tenant, the work starts. First, you will want to call your selected tenants and congratulate them on being selected for the property. Let them know what their possession date is and let them know that they should expect an e-mail or text with directions of what to have prepared for the day of possession. If they do not have email, ask for their mailing address so you can send the directions to them. We do not suggest going over it on the phone as people may write it down wrong or misunderstand your instructions.

Once you have secured your selected tenant and know that the person still have full intentions of moving into the place, you will need to call all the other potential tenants and let them know that you regret to have to inform them that you have selected another tenant. At this point, if the potential tenants are someone you still are interested in having, it is a good idea to ask them if they would like to know if you have or hear of any other properties that open up that may suit their needs. You never know if another property down the line or those of your friends could be a great fit for one of the potential tenants that you interviewed before. This will open up opportunities to joint venture with other investors with properties or simply save you time looking for a tenant for one of your other properties. Note that you also will need to return any initial deposits you have received from these potential tenants you have declined.

Now, you can concentrate on caring for your selected tenant. First thing we like to do is to refer back to our notes and see what the selected tenant likes. As part of our welcome package, we include a welcome binder and a welcome basket of goodies.

Welcome Binder

There are a few purposes of a welcome binder. These include looking professional and organized as well as ensuring that the tenants have one place where all their contracts and documents are. A welcome binder for us includes:

-   All contracts: Lease Agreement, Receipt of funds, pet applications, Utilities agreement

- A welcome letter
- A privacy statement, stating that their information is not sold
- Vacating Checklist Agreement
- Responsibilities and expectations
- Move in/move out inspections
- Bonuses to help tenants transition into the property:
  an amenities list of local spots that the tenants may want and a resource list.

You can adjust your welcome binder to include what you feel will suit your selected tenant. One of the most important parts we include in this binder is our expectations and their responsibilities. We will go over this in detail shortly. These documents should be reviewed by your lawyer so there are no legal issues.

Welcome Basket

The purpose of a welcome basket is pretty self-explanatory. Who doesn't like going into their new home and receiving a gift in the process? This also will help to smooth out the "agony" of filling out paperwork. After all the contracts and walk through, paper work is done, you can ask them to go through the welcome basket, which will leave them with a good feeling after you leave.

On the day of the possession, make sure the place is all clean and find a visible area to have your welcome binder, welcome basket and the keys for them. Greet your selected tenant outside and welcome them to their new home and then go inside with them. The goal is for their eyes to catch the welcome area and lead them there.

This is where you will introduce the welcome binder and welcome basket to them. You can then suggest doing the "boring" things like contracts first and then the fun stuff of the welcome basket. Most people are more than willing to take this approach.

Going through the Paperwork

At this time, you can go through all the contracts you have, as well as the move in and move out inspection walk through of the property. If you are not doing the contracts in triplicate on the day of possession, then make sure they get all copies within a week to be legally binding. Three copies are needed for: 1) your records, 2) the tenant's records and 3) your accountant. As we go through our welcome binder, we also go through the section on expectations and responsibilities. The reason we believe that this part is very important, if not the most important, is because it is the key to an easy management experience. Some of the key things we go through here are as follows:

-    Lawn maintenance and snow removal:

     o   Most people think that as managers, they will need to handle this. That is not necessarily the case as long as you make it very clear to the tenants. After all, who doesn't want a well-maintained lawn and clean driveway?

- Conflicts:

  o We let the tenants know that our expectations are that they try to resolve all conflicts themselves, and if it is still a problem, then to come to us. This is why it is important to properly screen a tenant in the first place. If you have done a good job of screening by using the methods we suggested in the previous chapters, you will tend to have fewer problems.

- Issues around the house:

  o Most people think that as managers, they will have to go fix a toilet in the middle of the night. While some people will opt to do it this way, we are aiming for an easy managing experience. To handle this, you will need a list of contacts who can respond to your calls to go to the property to fix things.

  o Have your tenants arrange a contractor of your choice to go to the property and get a quote. Make sure you have the contractor call you and give you a quote and tell you the reason why the issue occurred. By doing this you will not need to be the third person and play phone tag with your tenant and contractor to arrange a time. Also this allows you to make sure that the fix is necessary and how to prevent it. If the tenant caused the problem, it should be made known during the move in that it is their responsibility to take care of and pay for. Ex. Flushing something that doesn't belong, down the toilet.

o If your tenants are capable and willing to do the fixes themselves, make sure you ask them for a quote before they do anything. If you approve of the quote, remember to ask them for an invoice and also a receipt for any materials that was needed.

o If you get your tenant to do the fixes it is a good gesture to get them a bonus gift or gift certificate as a thank you. This will encourage them to take care of the property and also that you value them as your tenant. Only provide this gesture periodically, so it doesn't become an expectation.

Once contracts are done and you have received the checks, you also will need to do a move-in inspection. This is where you note any issues with the property with your tenants and mark it up so that when they move, you will know if the issues were pre-existing or if they were caused by your tenants. Note that this will have to be done again when your tenants move-out as a move out inspection. Allow your tenant all the time they want to record and comments or items during the walk through, you may also point out certain items for them to record to show that you understand that there is some wear and tear and that you are fair. After the walk through is complete let your tenant know that they will receive a copy of the walk through as soon as you can.

To assist you in this process, as a bonus to you we have included as a gift, our Document on Tenant Responsibilities and instant rental approval form. The instant rental approval form is a list of expectations and responsibilities that you as the landlord expects of the tenant. The tenant will go though the list and initial each item. This will ensure that the tenants has read and understood what the expectations are and what they have agreed to.

Please go to
www.makemoreworklessbook.com/cashflow for your gift.

Gift Time!

Now you can get on with the fun part and have them open up the welcome basket. This is probably our favorite part. The look of happiness on our tenant's faces as they discover what's in the welcome basket and open their gifts is awesome. We know at this point, that we have helped our tenant get into a nice home and have showed them that we care and want to make sure they are happy there. To make the experience a WOW for your tenants remember your previous conversations with your tenant when you are picking out their welcome gifts.

We're sure by now, you're wondering what should go in the welcome basket. This all goes back to when we said, put yourself in your tenant's shoes and think about what they would want when they first move in the place. It is a good idea to set yourself a budget and stay within it because it is easy to get carried away.

Some things we like to include in the basket are as follows:

- Shampoo, conditioner, hand soap and body wash
    o After a long day of moving, most people want to wash off the grime.
- Bath towel
- Key chains
- Garbage bags
- Shower curtains and rings
- Toilet paper
    o It's easy to forget to get toilet paper or have them packed away so well, you don't remember where it is.
- Paper towel
    o This is always handy when moving as you never know what messes you might have, especially if they are moving in when the weather is not cooperating!
- Coat hangers
- Snacks – chips, popcorn, candy
- Bottles of water
- Flowers and balloons
- Personal gifts
    o This is the extra touch we like to have to show our tenants that we were listening to their hobbies and what they like.
    o If during the meetings from before, your tenants have indicated to be big fans of hockey or a certain movie, it goes a long

way if you got them a hat with their favorite team or a movie with their favorite actor
- o Remember to get gifts to all members of the family even their pets. Getting toys for the kids, getting treats or toys for the pets will make their experience go the extra mile.
- o A nice gesture is to personalize each gift with their names
- o A dinner gift certificate is also a good idea, as after a long day of moving in, they can now relax and go out for dinner.
- o **BONUS TIP**: If the weather is hot, a box of frozen treats or ice cream in the freezer is a real crowd pleaser. If the weather is cold then hot chocolate makes a big difference.

This list varies for us depending on who the tenants are and whether it is just them or a family. Just as with screening a tenant, there is no science to this. Just put yourself in their shoes and think about what they may need or want when they are moving in it. Even if all the items in the welcome basket is self-explanatory, make sure you take the time to explain why and how the items will assist your tenants. Tell them why you picked the items you picked and word it as having your tenants in mind. For example: "And after a hard day's work of moving in, we would like you to relax without needing to find your towels and shampoo, we have provided that here for you. At the end of the day, when everything is in place we got you FREEZIES!"

After the welcome basket, you can welcome them to their new home again and then you are free to go and let them enjoy their new home.

Managing the Property and Tenant Long-Term

At the beginning of this chapter, we mentioned that managing properties the easy way also happens during the period of time when your tenants are renting from you. Have you ever experienced a situation where you have been a long-time client of a company, only to find out that they are offering all the good things to new clients and felt like you got the short end of the stick? Or perhaps, you saw a child that only got attention when he or she misbehaved. Why not treat your tenants good when they are treating you good by not calling you with problems? Little things you can do are to follow up with them once in a while to see how they are and if they have any concerns. This is where your notes will come in handy with remembering their kids or pets' names, their hobbies, what they were interested in, and so on. This shows your tenants that you care enough about them to listen and remember details about them.

Another way we like to treat our tenants well is during the holidays. While we are out shopping for our friends and families, we also get gifts for our tenants. We tend to have an appreciation gift for them once during the summer months and once again at Christmas time. This is another added bonus we feel happy about doing. How far you want to take this is entirely up to you. You can go so far as to send birthday cards for each of your tenants or calling them on special holidays to wish them a great day as well!

Always remember those who have helped you. If your tenant refers a potential tenant to you for another property, make sure you show your appreciation by getting them a thank-you card and gift certificate when that potential tenant becomes an actual tenant. This will encourage them to send more leads to you and also know that you value their tenancy.

As long as you start with a professional mindset and take the time and interest to care about your tenants, you will have a good relationship with your tenants. You will likely find that your tenants will have the respect you want from them.

Congratulations!

You have found, acquired, promoted, filled and are now managing your first rental property! All you need to do now is repeat what you have done, adjust and learn from your experience and accumulate more rental properties. The more you do, the more experience you get and the easier it gets! It will soon become your unconscious competence! Happy cashflow searching! You are well on your way to Make More and Work Less with Cashflow! As an extra Bonus to you for finishing this book, we would like to present you with our book:

Make More Work Less: The Guide to Unlocking Your Potential to Live and Work on Your Own Terms. Simply visit www.makemoreworklessbook.com/cashflow for your copy.

X	PARTNER
X	TENANT
X	CASHFLOW
X	PROPERTY
X	GOALS
X	VALUE
X	WOW

Have lists and be organized. Systems will allow you to do what you want to do with efficiency and reduce errors.

Chapter 14 – Managing Properties The Easy Way

Management is all about managing in the short term while developing the plans for the long-term.

- Jack Welch -

Assurance Keys to Your Success

- Treat your tenants great and you will have great tenants

- Congratulate your tenant and give clear instructions

- Welcome binder – professional and organized

- Make sure you voice your expectations and your tenant's responsibilities

- Complete a clear move-in walkthrough and go through paper work thoroughly

- Welcome Basket – What would you like to have when you first move in

- Personalized gifts to all members of the family

- Express how you value their tenancy

- Remember your tenants and make them feel special throughout their tenancy

275

- FINAL THOUGHTS -

Thank you for taking the time to read our book. We have put a lot of effort into this to make it a straightforward and an easily understood guideline on how to invest in cashflowing properties. We felt that by adding practical tips, we could give you the keys to the problems you could encounter to Make More and Work Less with Cashflow.

By now, you have already learned about the following:
1) Mindset
2) Acquiring properties
3) Maintaining relationships and properties

You might be thinking, "I read your book, what's next?" Well, that's a valid question. We've found all too often that a book, while comprehensive, sometimes leaves us with some questions we want answered. To help you move even further along, we have compiled interviews with our very own team members and coaches. Answers to frequently asked questions and tips are provided by our team and coaches so that you can have a better idea as to how to find a great team. To access these interviews please go to www.yourarea.ca.

If you have any questions you wish to have answered regarding this book, please feel free to e-mail us at makemoreworklessquestion@yourarea.ca. Please note that we get plenty of questions and e-mails daily, but we will do our best to answer your questions.

We will now leave you with one last quote from Dr. Phil. "Anyone can do something when they WANT to do it. Really successful people do things when they don't want to do it." So go out there and reach your dreams!

Thank you!

Recommended Book List

MINDSET
Change your mind Change your Results – Shawn Shewchuk
The Magic of Thinking Big – David Schwartz
Think and Grow Rich – Napoleon Hill
Who Moved My Cheese – Spencer Johnson
Stairway to Success – Nido Qubein

TIME MANAGEMENT
The Four Hour Work Week – Tim Ferriss

GOAL SETTING
Double Your Income Doing What You Love – Raymond Aaron

RELATIONSHIP BUILDING
How to Win Friends and Influence People – Dale Carnegie
Crucial Confrontations – Kerry Patterson, Joseph Grenny,
Ron McMillan and Al Switzler
Crucial Conversations – Kerry Patterson, Joseph Grenny,
Ron McMillan and Al Switzler
How to be a Great Communicator – Nido Qubein

REAL ESTATE/BUSINESS
Rich Dad Poor Dad – Robert Kiyosaki
Cashflow Quadrant – Robert Kiyosaki
Trump: Strategies for Real Estate – George Ross
Trump Style Negotiations – George Ross
Why We Want You To Be Rich – Robert Kiyosaki
and Donald Trump
Business Lessons from JT Foxx- JT Foxx
Pour Your Heart Into It – Howard Schultz
Onward – Howard Schultz
Walt Disney: An American Original – Bob Thomas

www.ingramcontent.com/pod-product-compliance
Lightning Source LLC
Chambersburg PA
CBHW061139220326
41599CB00025B/4299